# MOVING BEYOND TRAUMA

# MOVING

# BEYOND

# TRAUMA

The Roadmap to Healing from Your Past
and Living with Ease and Vitality

ILENE SMITH

**LIONCREST**
PUBLISHING

MOVING BEYOND TRAUMA
*The Roadmap to Healing from Your Past
and Living with Ease and Vitality*

ISBN   978-1-5445-0599-2 *Paperback*
      978-1-5445-0600-5 *Ebook*
      978-1-5445-0715-6 *Audiobook*

*This book is dedicated to my mentor Mia Elwood, and Healthy Futures AZ for the guidance and encouragement to take a deep dive into Somatic Experiencing and for giving me a home to practice my skills.*

# CONTENTS

INTRODUCTION ..............................................11

*Part One: Understanding the Mind-Body Connection*
1. MY JOURNEY TO HEALING ............................ 25
2. YOU ARE NOT YOUR BRAIN .......................... 43
3. TRAUMA: WE'VE ALL GOT IT ........................ 73
4. WHAT HEALING LOOKS LIKE ...................... 107

*Part Two: Creating Change*
5. ASSESSING YOUR PROBLEM BEHAVIORS ........147
6. HEALING EXERCISES.................................. 207
7. LIVING A HEALING LIFESTYLE.................... 223

CONCLUSION ............................................. 237
REFERENCES .............................................241
ACKNOWLEDGMENTS ................................. 249
ABOUT THE AUTHOR.................................251

# INTRODUCTION

On some level, albeit often a subconscious one, people realize that their bodies and minds are intricately connected. Look no further than yoga or Pilates. Often, people begin these practices based on the physical results they want to achieve. But if they stick with them for long enough, something starts to change. You will often hear practitioners talk about how the physical movement "alleviates stress" or "eases their mind." This is not a coincidence. It's the mind-body connection at work. What these people are actually experiencing is the dawning understanding that we don't handle stress in our heads, for as much as Western society treats stress as a cognitive issue. In truth, healing and balance require bringing the body into the process.

*Psychological stress is held and manifests in our physical body.* It's important to understand this, because in this day and age the vast majority of us are experiencing increasing levels of stress as the world becomes a little bit faster every single day. As more mental health issues crop up, people are beginning to understand that the things we're currently doing, including different types of talk therapy, don't offer the complete solution. Even insurance companies are starting to acknowledge this by contributing to alternative therapies and preventative care.

Since you picked up this book, you may very well be in the same position that so many of my clients find themselves in: you've tried all of the traditional routes to resolve psychological stress and trauma, yet you are still in the thick of it. Perhaps you've tried therapy or even medication and you still feel anxious or dysregulated. Maybe you feel like your body and brain are moving in different directions. If so, you're not alone.

We are told that psychological issues are resolved in our head—that it's a cognitive process. As a Somatic Experience therapist, I couldn't disagree more. Have you ever heard the phrase "We hold our issues in our tissues?" It's something like that. To feel less stress, more connection, more joy, and more healed, we *have* to bring our bodies into the equation. That's where the answers lie, and *that* is the missing link.

## HOW YOU GOT HERE

Most people go to talk therapy because they want their life to feel different somehow. They want to feel more comfortable, more connected to the people and world around them and to themselves. They want to feel safer.

Through the process of talk therapy, we dig around and try to understand *why* the things in our lives are the way they are; why *we* are the way we are. We seek answers for why we act the way we do, why certain things are so difficult, and why we can't achieve the things in life we want to achieve, such as healthy, loving relationships, a sense of autonomy, or a feeling of fulfillment. We go to talk therapy because we're curious about ourselves and want to make a change for the better. We want answers.

All of this is very well intentioned. After all, it's what we're told to do when we want to improve our lives and ourselves. Don't get me wrong: I do believe that talk therapy certainly offers some benefits. However, here is the issue: in the process of digging around for answers, most therapeutic processes end up dredging up our past experiences. And when we talk through those experiences without also dealing with them in an embodied way, talk therapy can actually be counterproductive. We can end up re-traumatizing ourselves rather than healing. Instead of healing, we move into more discomfort—or, at least, our level of discomfort does not diminish. As human beings, our natural instinct is to move away from pain, so very few people actually dive into and resolve the pain that can be brought up in the course of talk therapy.

We can't trick our bodies into thinking we've dealt with pain and trauma simply by talking through it. We might be able to fool our mind, but we can't fool our body—and we *especially* can't fool our nervous system.

Processing and expunging the pain and trauma of past experience is like peeling back the layers of an onion. One of the things we must do in this process is to build up resilience. We need to build up a new sense of safety. Without doing these things, we have not resolved the issues we sought out therapy for in the first place.

There are certain things you can do along the way to help you build up a better sense of safety and connection. For example, I have many clients who have attended various types of healing workshops. For a lot of them, those workshops have been helpful insofar as they have helped create connection and a sense of safety. Both of these things are very important. But they still don't solve the problem on a root level. They just take care of one layer of it. In order to get to the root of our pain, hurt, and trauma and heal it once and for all, we have to bring our body and nervous system into the process. It's how we are built as human beings.

I also have to tell you that there is no quick fix for any of this. Healing is possible, but it takes time. However, I know plenty of people who have spent years and years in talk therapy—I spent fifteen years in it myself—and never found true healing.

As a society, we have become accustomed to quick fixes and distractions. We can just turn to our phones and listen to a podcast or scroll mindlessly through social media until we have managed to blunt whatever emotion it is that we are trying to avoid. We can look at porn, we can shop, we can play games—we have an enormous toolbox of distractions at our fingertips these days. More than ever before in the history of mankind, we don't have to sit with our emotions if we don't want to. Because, let's be honest, who really *wants* to sit with some of the more difficult human emotions like grief, anger, and sadness?

Despite our best intentions, talk therapy can be a distraction too. It distracts us from what we're feeling. It keeps us focused on trying to solve the problem or level up, so to speak. What it doesn't do, though, is get to the heart of the issue at hand. It does not hold our hand so that we can safely move through whatever it is we are feeling and get to the other side.

## WHAT TALK THERAPY DOES AND DOESN'T DO

I *wanted* to heal long before I actually did. In fact, I spent years and years trying to heal, but I now realize that despite all of my best efforts, I just didn't have the tools at my disposal to do so. Like so many people, I thought that talk therapy would provide me with all of the answers I needed to understand my pain and behavior and, thus, how to bring an end to both of them. I continued to believe this even after years of continuing talk therapy without any significant changes in my behavior or how I felt.

I want to be clear that it's not that I didn't gain anything out of talk therapy; I did. I learned a lot about how I functioned as a human being. Talk therapy opened my eyes to the fact that I was afraid of setting boundaries, and avoided situations that made me uncomfortable. I tended to shift between over-attaching and detaching to the people in my life. In short, talk therapy gave me a framework through which I could recognize when things weren't right or when I wasn't behaving in ways that worked toward my best interests. But it didn't help me break these habits or maladaptive behaviors. It just made me more aware of them.

Awareness does help some things. For example, I used to be an emotional eater with disordered eating patterns. Therapy helped me become aware of the fact that I had the tendency to use food as a way of avoiding feelings of loneliness. I started doing this as a kid; when I walked into an empty house, I would immediately go into the kitchen. This behavior continued into my adult life. By then, it was habit.

Thanks to therapy, as an adult I became aware of and subsequently corrected that behavior. Now, when I walk into an empty house, I don't allow myself to go into the kitchen first, because I understand that acts as a trigger for me. I changed the behavior and broke the habit. Here's the thing, though: changing the behavior did not change my nervous system's reaction to being alone, it just changed my pattern for dealing with that loneliness. It's the same for all of us. Even if we can change a pattern or behavior through therapy, unless we are dealing with the issue from the bottom up (in other words, by bringing our body into the picture), it will show up elsewhere.

For me, not walking into the kitchen didn't change the fact that I felt lonely, couldn't sleep well, and tried to soothe myself by zoning out and watching mindless television. The root issue was still there, unaddressed. I still felt uncomfortable in my body based on my nervous system's reaction.

The other tricky thing about talk therapy is that, by nature, it requires you to keep telling your story over and over and over. This keeps calling upon pain and, furthermore, engrains the story more deeply into your identity. Pain isn't resolved from the neck up. We hold the trauma of our stories in our entire body, so our pain and trauma have to be resolved systemically in our bodies. Cognitive relief does not help reconnect us to our sensory experience. Just talking about our experiences does not provide us with a sense of mastery or a feeling of completion and safety. Additionally, retelling the story can reactivate our trauma.

Talk therapy can provide insight and help you understand how your past experiences are impacting your life today. That's a good thing. These verbal stories may very well lead you to understand the story that is playing out in your body, reiterating its experience in your nervous system. In that way, talk therapy can serve as a useful roadmap. However, talk therapy alone will never be a complete solution.

## SOMATIC THERAPY

When I found Somatic Experiencing (SE) therapy, I still sometimes found myself feeling anxious and uncomfortable, but I didn't know what to do to resolve that. I still had difficulty feeling calm and centered in certain moments. Other times, I found myself being reactive, didn't feel fully connected to myself or others, or present. I noticed that anxiety crept in at times and places when

I would have least expected it. For example, no matter how much talk therapy I did, the second I sensed that I wasn't being heard, I immediately disconnected from the person I was communicating with and went offline. I understood rationally that this behavior wasn't effective, but I still couldn't do anything to change it.

SE is a body-based therapeutic modality that does include talking but utilizes talking as a window in, to track and notice body sensations and experiences. From there, the individual can safely move through the traumatizing experience, thus unsticking the energy from their body in order to heal. SE allowed me to heal, connect with, and build a relationship with myself through my body rather than my brain. In doing this, I was finally able to react to myself, my world, and my experiences in new ways. From there, I began to gain a deeper capacity to stay connected to other people and to the world around me. It allowed me to socially engage so that I could be supported. In the years that have followed, as I have offered this same therapy to my own clients, I have seen them experience similar shifts—shifts that are nothing short of transformative. Shifts that completely eluded them, no matter how many years they dedicated to talk therapy before coming to SE.

Learning how to experience this sort of connection with self and with others changes everything, and it does so relatively quickly as compared to talk therapy. Whereas I was in talk therapy for twenty years with very little effect, within less than six months I started to notice the difference with Somatic Experiencing. This is because rather than working through my brain, SE addressed something talk therapy never had: my nervous system. This is critical, because our nervous system is way smarter than our brain. No amount of cognitive work is ever going to be able to override what your nervous system is telling you is truth. For example, you can tell yourself that you are comfortable engaging with people, but if anxiety is cropping up in your body every time you engage with another person, how effective is that engagement really going to be? How connected will you actually feel? How safe?

Whereas I used to be constantly activated and everything always seemed catastrophic before SE, today nothing is. I can flow through life with more fluidity and am not in a constant state of reaction to the world. I don't feel the need to control things that are beyond my control.

Of course, I am human, so I still have my moments. But because I am attuned with my body and, specifically, my nervous system, I know when there is too much stimulation and I can't tolerate it anymore. At that point, I can make the decision to withdraw, rather than engaging in an ultimately unproductive and potentially harmful way.

I see the same difference I saw in myself in my clients all of the time. Somatic Experiencing helps them to understand their trauma from a new perspective, from the perspective of their body rather than their head. I find that even the act of helping clients understand why their bodies and minds often work in opposition with one another creates a new, safer container in which to heal, and helps to alleviate some of the shame of what they are dealing with. They can begin to let go of some of the whys: "*Why* do I do this?" "*Why* am I stuck in this place?"

Instead, SE gives us permission to notice without judgment. With this understanding, clients can become their own observer and begin to lean into their discomfort in order to ultimately move through it. For as scary as it might sound, as soon as we lean in and let go of the anxiety that often accompanies feeling the pressure to find a solution, the nervous system begins to settle down. As clients become more and more able to lean into their discomfort, they simultaneously build more and more resilience. They begin to understand that it's okay to feel bad sometimes. It's *human* to feel bad sometimes. And, ultimately, allowing yourself to feel bad, rather than using food, drugs, alcohol and other types of destructive avoidance behavior, is not only more productive, but it also offers more freedom and feels better in the long run.

As time goes by, clients begin to realize that the emotional pain and discomfort that manifests in their body won't kill them. By simply being there with it and building more resilience rather than trying to avoid or logic their way through it, people ultimately begin to build a deeper relationship with themselves, build more connection, and experience the world in a new way. Their attachments become healthier and the world feels less dangerous.

Clients often describe the feeling that comes with this as experiencing life in a more comfortable or focused way. Things seem less chaotic, and they feel less stressed. This works equally well and is equally transformative for someone who experiences mild depression and anxiety or someone who is grappling with the effects of PTSD.

True healing is a journey. There is no quick fix. But as you learn to build resilience and connection to yourself and others throughout the coming pages, you will learn how to incorporate practices into your life that will usher you along this healing path. You will begin to peel back the layers of your pain one by one and, in the process, draw closer to your true self.

Throughout the course of this book, I invite you to be your own observer. I invite you not to tell your story, but to notice what's happening in your body *right now*. That is the first piece of moving out of discomfort and into a freer life.

# PART ONE

# UNDERSTANDING THE MIND-BODY CONNECTION

———

# CHAPTER ONE

# MY JOURNEY TO HEALING

Traditional Western therapy believes in strong boundaries between therapist and client. The underlying reasons for this are straightforward. However, this approach does not allow for a two-way connection. It does not allow patients to understand that their therapists are *also* human, and that the only difference between the therapist and the client is that the therapist has learned to utilize tools—the same tools they are passing on to the client.

While I believe that the focus should always remain on the client in a therapeutic setting, I also believe there should be a two-way connection, and that it can be helpful for clients to understand that their therapist is no different from them and has worked through their own share of pain and trauma. In fact, it is from this experiential place that they can counsel. As a clinician, I believe you can only take clients as far as you are willing to go yourself.

For this reason, I often share the following story with my clients. And then I explain how I was able to get there.

I tell them that the morning of June 18, 2016 started out just like any other. I woke up super early in the morning and couldn't fall back asleep, which is not uncommon for me. Giving up on sleep, I got out of bed and walked out to the den. About twenty minutes later, my husband Bill walked in and asked in the sweetest way, "Does anyone need a snuggle?"

I went running back into the bedroom and, within three seconds of being in my husband's arms, I fell back asleep until the alarm went off a couple of hours later. When I woke up later that morning, I remember telling Bill, "That was the best snuggle ever!"

Bill got out of bed and started getting ready for a sailing regatta that he was participating in. It was a few days into the regatta and, at this point in the race, Bill's boat was winning. He was really excited, despite the fact that his stomach had been hurting him for the past couple of days.

As Bill continued getting ready to sail, I kissed him goodbye and we both said, "I love you." I watched him walk into the bathroom as I headed out the door to meet with my cycling group of about twenty people to go for a ride.

A couple of hours later, I was on my bike and my phone kept ringing. I looked down and saw that I had several missed calls, including calls from both a guy who Bill sailed with and someone from his office. Clearly, people were trying to track me down. My first thought was, "Oh, my God. I hope Bill didn't get hurt on his boat!"

"I have to stop," I shouted out to no one in particular.

At this point, I don't even remember who I called back first, but I know that whoever it was told me that Bill had never shown up to the regatta that morning. He also didn't show up for the breakfast he was supposed to go to before that. I called our apartment and there was no answer. I called our doorman and asked him to go up to our apartment to see if Bill was there.

By this point, I already knew that Bill was dead. I can't explain why I knew; I just did. I had had a recurring premonition for the previous six months that he was going to die, despite the fact that I had no logical reason for thinking this. As part of these premonitions, I felt strongly that Bill would die in our apartment in Chicago, and that I wouldn't be there when it happened. In the past few weeks, these premonitions had taken on a mounting intensity and frequency.

My last premonition had occurred just the night before, when Bill and I were walking to dinner. I happened to glance back to where Bill was walking behind me. As I looked at him, I saw death in his eyes. I don't know how to explain it other than that. Also, on that particular night, as we drove down a street we had driven down at least fifty times before, Bill pointed out a building where he had lived with his dad after college. Rarely had Bill talked about his dad, and he had certainly never shown me that building.

Sure enough, when the doorman entered our apartment, he found Bill lying on the bathroom floor, unresponsive. We did not perform an autopsy for religious reasons, but, piecing things together, I am fairly certain that Bill died of an abdominal aneurysm.

It took more than an hour to get back to Chicago, but I don't even remember the Uber ride, except for calling my parents. I was filled with dread at the thought of having to break the news to them, because they loved Bill.

### DEALING WITH BILL'S DEATH

Bill was the love of my life. We got married later in life— just six years before his death at age sixty-five—but I had always expected that Bill and I would have much more time together than we did.

Still, I never freaked out about Bill's death. I attribute this to the fact that I had already done so much work on myself and with Bill prior to his death. During our time together, Bill and I were on a mutual, powerful journey of growth, which included SE (and thank God for that!). Now, we are continuing on that journey together; it's just not the journey we had envisioned.

I would have never believed it beforehand, but I was able to move through the pain and discomfort of Bill's death while still remaining connected with the world around me. This, for me, was unprecedented. I had a long history of not allowing people to support me. Probably in large part because of this newfound ability to remain in a state of connection even in a time of despair; I also never lost sight of the fact that, despite the fact that losing Bill was horribly painful, in the long run I was going to be okay.

While I loved Bill deeply, our relationship was not perfect. We had issues, including the fact that Bill's moods were often unpredictable, which sometimes made me feel unsafe in the relationship. I also came into the relationship with my own set of anxieties. Before I met Bill, I had spent those fifteen years in therapy, trying to resolve this one issue: the massive amount of fear and anxiety I constantly carried around about losing my parents. Despite all of the therapy, I never grappled with or moved beyond that fear. Instead, when I married Bill the fear transferred onto him. Bill and I were both willing to do the work we needed to do both on our own and as a couple to allow our relationship to thrive, so we began a journey of growth together.

Although each of our fears are unique, I think there is a common expectation (often subconsciously) that the person who we marry will heal all the pieces of us that are broken. Of course, that doesn't happen, so then comes disenchantment, often followed by a cycle of attempts at repairing that disenchantment, and perhaps retraumatization.

Bill and I spent the first couple of years of our relationship retraumatizing one another, with each of us blaming the other for not getting what we needed. Then, finally, we each learned to take responsibility for ourselves. From there, we were able to create a new, far more solid foundation than the one we originally had. We were able to build a safe container for our relationship. Don't get me wrong, this was challenging. But the beautiful thing is, we were both able to do the work, both together and separately.

Amazingly, it is because of this work that I was able to deal and heal when my greatest fear was actually realized. I could have blamed Bill for leaving me. I could have disconnected from others and from myself and my own painful feelings. I could have fallen into anxiety. I could have fallen back into destructive habits. At previous points in my life, I would have done all of these things. But this time I didn't. Even in the midst of the biggest crisis and loss of my life, I was able to remember that my body organically knew what to do and practice what SE taught me. And here's why: through my work and the practice of SE, I was finally able to get to a place in life and within myself where I felt safe. Once I felt safe, I was able to tolerate the discomfort I experienced around my core issues, including the biggest issue of all: attachment. I was able to process my painful emotions in a way that was productive and healthy. I didn't try to run or shut down like I always had before. I wasn't afraid of my own feelings, no matter how devastating they were at certain moments.

Here is what my life looked like after Bill died. The morning after he died, I distinctly remember thinking, "Oh, my God. This pain is so intense I can barely get out of bed." Nonetheless, I made a conscious decision to move through that pain and sorrow with the hope that maybe there would be a point when Bill wouldn't be the first thing I thought about when I got up in the morning. I did not do this by going into a state of shock or numbness. I allowed myself to feel every bit of the pain I was in so that I could allow it to move through me. To do that, I understood that I needed support, both from myself and from others. For the first three months after Bill died, I made sure I had dinner plans every night. I kept myself engaged in and with the world. After a few months, I left Chicago (where Bill's business had been and where we spent our summers), and returned to our home in Phoenix, where I felt I could better delve into my own work.

The most important thing to notice here is that none of this means that I didn't experience the pain of grief. In fact, I *fully* experienced the pain. I allowed myself to feel all of it. And I also allowed myself to find and experience moments of joy even in the midst of grieving, which was just as important. So often in life, whether it's because of grief or any other variety of trauma or emotional or psychological pain, we believe that we can only have one or the other, joy or pain. More accurately, we believe that we can only have one at the expense of the other. This is not true. We can—and are meant to—have many emotions and experiences all at once. That's part of the human experience and how we are built. I remember laughing the week after Bill died. There were plenty of moments when I cried, too, but I had the capacity for both. Because I allowed myself to have both and because I refused to isolate either myself or my feelings, my nervous system found a way to not only survive, but to thrive even in the midst of trauma and the unknown.

All of this was possible because I lost Bill at a point when my nervous system was regulated. I wasn't sensing the world as a dangerous place. Instead, I sensed the world as a place of support. I knew that the world had resources to offer me, and I knew that I had resources within myself that I could utilize to get through the pain and loss of his death.

Bill's death represented my greatest fear come to fruition. I believe that it is when we are placed right in the middle of the most adverse experiences life has to present us with that we have the opportunity to build the most resilience for ourselves. It is during these times when we have the opportunity to build a sense of mastery around our own experience and to realize: I can make it through.

## BATTLING MY BODY

I have an acute understanding of why my clients are so reluctant to be in their body, with their pain. I spent years in a constant state of battle with my body.

I was raised in an upper-middle-class, first-generation Jewish family. There were a lot of epigenetics at play and a lot of neuroses came with that. My parents didn't know how to communicate, and they didn't know how to raise kids. There was a pretty constant stream of yelling and screaming in my childhood home.

At age six, I called a sleepaway camp and signed myself up for an eight-week session. I was trying to do whatever

I could to get out of all of that chaos. I vividly remember lying in bed at just nine years old, listening to my parents fight. I was so scared, and I couldn't stop crying, thinking how horrible all of this was. I didn't feel safe. The constant state of turmoil in my house was exacerbated by the fact that I had a series of eye surgeries when I was very young—between the ages of one-and-a-half and three years old—and carried with me a lot of fear from that. Although I wouldn't have explained it that way at the time, my nervous system was on overdrive throughout the course of my childhood.

I should also say that, despite the chaos and how it impacted me, my family was not short on love. I was constantly told how much I was loved, and I *felt* loved. But I didn't feel safe, despite what I'm sure were all of the good intentions in the world.

I expressed this overdrive by quite literally keeping myself in constant motion; I was always active and spent much of my spare time running. When we are children, our little bodies are so intuitive. Of course, I didn't understand what I was doing at the time, but I can now clearly see that I was trying to regulate my dysregulated nervous system however I could. I had a hard time concentrating and couldn't absorb information, so I wasn't a great student. There was no one there to hold my hand through all of this. Then body shame set in when I was in my teens because I was such a late bloomer.

What I *did* have amidst all of this were great survival instincts. I was smart, so I knew how to survive, whether it was through moving or getting notes for class from someone who did know how to pay attention.

I had a lot of maladaptive behaviors, too. By the time I was a freshman in college I was anorexic, constantly over-exercising, and practicing a lot of strange behaviors around food that were designed to restrict my intake. I couldn't get comfortable within myself. The more I tried to somehow create a connection or sense of comfort within my body, the deeper into the trauma vortex I fell. I now understand that I thought the way to reconcile myself with my body and to get comfortable was by somehow making it "perfect." I thought this would resolve my sense of shame and chaos. The more I tried to do that, the worse I felt about myself and my body. I knew something wasn't right, but I didn't know how to fix it, much less how to get to the root of it.

It felt like my body was a prison and I was locked inside of it. Everything in my life revolved around how I felt about my body at any given moment in time. If I got my exercise in (and, by that, I mean an eight-mile run or a forty-mile bike ride), ate a certain way, and everything else was "in order," then I could function in the world in a calmer way. But if those pieces weren't in place—and, let me tell you, it took a lot of physical, mental, and emotional effort to keep those pieces in place—then nothing else was in place, either. My sense of self-worth wasn't, nor were my relationships or sense of safety.

It was all very rigid and, because of this, to the outside eye it looked like I had my shit together. What people were really seeing was a lot of dysregulation.

After years and years of trying to fight this behavior, only to be defeated by the sense of wanting to crawl out of my own skin, I finally found relief in SE. But first, I had to be willing to sit in that feeling of discomfort I had been running from for so long.

Before I found SE, I found mindfulness. For me, that was an important first step to body awareness. Many years into talk therapy, I asked my therapist why I still felt so anxious and uncomfortable. It was then that he told me about John Kabat-Zinn's studies on mindfulness-based meditation. Kabat-Zinn is a Harvard professor who ran the first study on mindful-based stress reduction, also known as MSBR. His studies showed that mindfulness-based interventions improved both mental and physical health more effectively than psychological interventions. These studies ultimately formed the basis for an institute at Mass General Hospital, which Kabat-Zinn now runs.

By that point, I was willing to try whatever might work, so I immediately purchased a meditation cushion and one of John Kabat-Zinn's CD meditations. I started with a five-minute meditation and built up to ten minutes. Eventually, I got to the point where I could sit for twenty minutes two times a day. With this came a noticeable decrease in my level of anxiety.

I was intrigued, so I decided to do a week-long meditation workshop in MSBR. I was really into it, *except* for the body-scan meditation, which I had avoided like the plague on the CDs. At the retreat, though, I was stuck. The body-scan meditation lasted for an hour and it was brutal. It quickly made me realize how out of touch with my body I actually was. The meditation leader told us to feel our feet, and I realized I *couldn't* feel my foot. I knew it was there and that I could move it, but I couldn't *feel* it. I was completely disconnected from my body. As soon as the body scan ended, the group broke for lunch and my immediate response was to go for a hard four-mile run. It was the only way I could think of to settle my nervous system. It was then that I had an epiphany that changed everything: I could only feel my body when I was in pain. This got me curious. I began to wonder, "*Is* there a way for me to be in my body and feel joy?" I was in my forties when this happened, and it was an entirely new thought for me.

I would soon find my answer. I was completing my master's in mental health, and my internship placement was in a center for eating disorders. It was the first work environment where I had ever felt totally safe. Nothing was a problem, it was all a learning experience. One day, I expressed this to the founder of the clinic, Mia, who was also my supervisor. She explained that many of the clinicians were trained in SE, and encouraged me to take the beginning training. I had no idea what I was getting into when I embarked upon these three years of intense training, but I knew that I wanted more of this: more of this sense of safety, more joy, and more presence. It was during this training that a light bulb went off for me as I started to learn about how trauma embeds itself in the body, impacting the nervous system.

Author Eckhart Tolle says that there are two types of emotional pain we carry in our body: the pain we carry from our past, and the pain we create in our present. This pain is the primary source of all drama, pain, and suffering in humanity. I think what Tolle means by this is that our experience in this present moment in time is vastly impacted by our cumulative experiences up to this point. When we have unresolved trauma, it becomes locked in our body and impacts our present experience. I'm sure you've been in a situation in the past when you've said something seemingly innocuous to a person and they have lost it. This is their accumulated pain talking. It is the manifestation of someone sensing danger not because of you, but because of a memory. You just happen to be the unknowing trigger. Of course, all of this happens on a subconscious level.

Although this is a subconscious process, our body often clues us in to that lingering emotional pain, just as my body did on that run during the mindfulness retreat. With the dawning awareness that I could not feel my body unless it was in pain, my mind began to track back. I realized that, as a child, feeling pain in my body was a survival mechanism. It was only when I felt pain or was sick that I received attention. It was when I felt safe. Then there was this other piece, too, which was that my mom was always really scared of everything. On a deep level I knew that if I inherited this sense of fear, I wouldn't be able to do anything—and so, instead of potentially feeling that fear, I disconnected from my body. And, thus, I entered into a decades-long cycle of alternating between not allowing myself to feel my body most of the time, then triggering pain so that I could feel—but only in a specific way.

Once I began Somatic Experiencing, two things began to happen very quickly. First, when I did start to exercise, my body became overstimulated very quickly. I had created a connection with my body, so I was now able to hear it when it told me, "That's not good." The other thing that happened is that I was also able to hear my body when it felt good. I could tell that, when I moved gently, my body responded by feeling calmer.

## WHAT HEALING LOOKS LIKE

Understanding all of this was one thing. Putting it into practice was another. I built resilience within my body to open up and sit with pain. This is a scary prospect. At first, I allowed myself to feel that pain in small amounts, then for a bit longer, and then a bit longer still. For as much as I didn't love opening myself up to emotional pain, I also couldn't help but notice how much my life began changing for the better once I did. I also came to realize that pain isn't permanent—at least, it's not if we feel it and allow it the space to move through us. I also began to see that I could be in charge of my life, rather than trying to control outside factors to gain a false sense of being in control.

Over time, I put the tools I'll show you in this book to use. I reconnected with my body in a healthy way. I listened to what it told me it was feeling, good, bad, or otherwise. I sat with my feelings until they reached their natural conclusion. Slowly and over time, I learned that my body was capable of moving through pain in healthy ways, so that I could become unstuck. All of this might sound like a lot but, as you put these tools into use, I think you'll begin to find—as many of my clients do—that it all starts to feel effortless. Your body and nervous system want to return to their natural state of health. It's just up to you to provide the space for that to happen.

I am human. I don't love it when I feel sad or lonely or scared. But now I also understand that I am having these feelings for a reason. They are telling me something that I need to hear. They are moving me forward. And when I listen, they say their piece and move on, making space for me to fully be there for whatever other feelings and experiences follow. I can tell you honestly that, for as full of fear and detached from myself as I once was, I am no longer like that.

I changed, evolved, and came more fully alive. I feel and understand joy and connection in ways I never could have before. And, I promise you that if I can do it, so can you.

# CHAPTER TWO

# YOU ARE NOT YOUR BRAIN

When we think of psychology, it generally conjures up images of Freud and analysis. We think of it as an almost entirely verbal and cognitive process.

When I first introduce the idea of body-based psychology to people, I have to help them understand that while it focuses on the nervous system, it is not entirely non-verbal. However, the emphasis is different from what we are currently programmed to expect in therapeutic settings. While talk therapy breaks down the story, Somatic Experiencing breaks down and examines the way in which our story impacts our body. In other words, talking will only get you so far in body-based psychology. In SE, we view the body as the primary communicator. To heal, it's our job to listen because the body can tell us things that words never could.

## TOP-DOWN THERAPY

Those forms of therapy we are most familiar with in the modern world—psychodynamic (more commonly known as talk therapy), cognitive behavioral therapy (CBT), and dialectical behavioral therapy (DBT)—are all top-down approaches. They teach people to change their thoughts and behaviors. While this approach may have some surface-level efficacy, it does not get to the root of the problem. It fails to address the underlying piece that needs to be healed.

Top-down therapy *does* have a place. I do believe there is some value in understanding our own story and also in feeling heard by another person. So many times, trauma occurs simply because a person feels unheard. I know that I have benefitted from that sense of having a witness in the course of talk therapy. However, the real goal with therapy is to live a better, more peaceful, fulfilled, and connected life *moving forward*. And that is the piece that talk therapy often misses—arming clients with an understanding of how their past impacts their lives today and, most importantly, how to alleviate that rather than causing retraumatization by re-living painful past experiences. So, while talk therapy does serve a purpose, in my opinion it is only part of the puzzle. Patients might use it to gain witness, insight, and to put voice to their story, but it should not be the only or final step in healing.

These days, psychodynamic therapy, CBT, and DBT are

the most common forms of therapy, largely because insurance supports them. In psychodynamic therapy, the patient is guided toward free association thoughts in an attempt to bring unconscious patterns of behavior into their awareness. CBT is a type of exposure therapy that is used a lot with people with anxiety and phobias. It is a highly cognitive process that moves patients even further away from their bodies than they likely were to begin with. Essentially, it exposes patients to whatever they are triggered by and attempts to encourage new behavior within that. The problem is that, for obvious reasons, CBT can be retraumatizing. DBT assists patients with emotional regulation, distress tolerance, interpersonal skills, and mindfulness. Of all the talk therapies, I find DBT to be the most effective because it regulates the nervous system and draws patients closest to their current experience.

Politics and insurance play a large role in the popular therapies of any given moment. For example, there was a lot of research about psychedelic drugs as a healing therapy in the 1960s, but that all came to a halt beginning with the Nixon administration and continuing with the Reagan administration's Say No to Drugs campaign. Insurance will only support evidence-based treatments, so it's no accident that the most common forms of top-down therapies have all been subject to research studies. The problem is that these studies don't necessarily tell us everything we need to know, so they can provide a skewed view of their efficacy. For example, CBT might do a wonderful job of reducing some of the maladaptive behaviors involved with eating disorders. But do those patients then begin to drink more? In other words, these studies only look at one specific marker, rather than the holistic benefit a therapy has on a person's overall quality of life. We are not measuring how patients' relationships with themselves and with other people in their lives change as a result of therapy. If someone is no longer practicing disordered eating, but is still miserable, I would argue they are not actually healed at all even if, according to research markers, they are.

Only recently have advances in neuroscience begun to prove the efficacy of body-based therapies and the body-mind connection, and thus to build a large body of work around it. And, here's the thing: the common denominator between all of these top-down therapies is that they involve the brain's ability to override the body—and it can't. Not in the long-term. Pain does not exist in our head; it exists in our body.

In addition to the more logistical reasons why talk therapy is considered to be the primary avenue for psychological healing today, societal norms also come into play. In the Western world, we have been conditioned not to feel. A lot of us aren't even aware of the degree to which we avoid feeling. For example, when a child cries, a parent's first instinct is often to distract them; to stop the crying. Instead, we could wrap that child up in our arms to provide them with a safe place to have that experience of sadness, discomfort, or distress. We have become uncomfortable with feeling, whether it is us or someone else experiencing emotion. Because we don't allow ourselves to fully experience our emotions in the first place, we also don't know how to see those feelings through or how to self-soothe.

Top-down therapy does not move us any closer toward this. In fact, this underlying question of "Why?" moves us *away* from feeling. It is because of this learned ability to feel that I was able to see myself through my husband's death so successfully. I *allowed* myself to be with my feelings, rather than repressing them or making my grief a mental exercise.

While all of this is important to note, it's also not to say that there is no place for these top-down therapies. DBT, for example, is a great adjunct to the type of somatic therapy we will be discussing in this book, because it assists with emotional regulation, distress tolerance, interpersonal skills, and mindfulness. It is, essentially, all about a person's relationship with themselves and with others. The mindfulness piece helps patients regulate their nervous system and bring them into their body. Most of all, DBT is not limited to the time a client spends in a therapist's office; it is a *practice* meant to be brought into day-to-day life. But, even at that, it's still not enough.

## BOTTOM-UP THERAPY

As you can probably guess from the name alone, Somatic Experiencing, or bottom-up therapy, works in almost the reverse way of top-down therapy. Rather than concentrating on changing thoughts and behaviors, it addresses the ways in which a patient senses the world. It works with the fight, flight, or freeze mechanics that live in our nervous system in such a way that we can ultimately resolve and heal our hurts on a deep level. With this, our behaviors will still ultimately change, but they change as a result of the healing that has occurred on a systematic level. In other words, bottom-up therapy offers an organic process of change rather than a forced process.

The other big benefit to bottom-up therapy is that it allows people to address issues that occur during their pre-verbal years—issues that they could never even begin to address in top-down therapy, because they are inaccessible through cognitive memory (more on this shortly). With bottom-up therapy, a person's body is able to guide them to the root of these early-life issues and incidents through symptoms like body rigidity and incomplete reflexes.

Another big difference between top-down and bottom-up therapy is that there are strict guidelines against touching in traditional talk therapy. These exist to maintain professional boundaries between therapists and their clients, with the very good intention of providing a safe environment in which the client can heal and work through issues.

What this guideline fails to consider, however, is that touch is an innate need of human beings and a powerful tool for healing.[1] It makes sense when you think about it: touch is the first human sense to develop in utero; it is at the very foundation of our composition. In the womb, we are enveloped in amniotic fluid. This fluid cradles and nurtures us, providing a sense of safety and protection. This feeling of being physically cocooned is a universal experience of coming online as a human. In fact, it marks the beginning of the development of our nervous system.

We are quite literally designed for touch. The inability to experience this essential need as the result of either acute or chronic trauma is detrimental to the health of our nervous system and our ability to connect with others and the world around us. Reestablishing a client's capacity to experience touch is essential to healing and an integral part of successful therapy. This is all but impossible to accomplish in a modality that prohibits touch.

---

1   "Hands on Research: The Science of Touch" by Dacher Keltner, *Greater Good Magazine*; September 29, 2010.

Touch healing can look a number of different ways in a therapeutic environment. I work with some clients who have experienced so much trauma around touch that even the *idea* of it is threatening. I have a client named Emily who fell firmly into this category. When she first came to me, Emily was quite dysregulated and, with that, extremely averse to touch.

It took several months for Emily and me to build a foundation of trust and for her to come to the understanding that she is not alone in the world, and there are safe places in life. It wasn't until six months into our work that we built up enough resources for Emily to reach the point where she was willing to begin working with touch. The first time Emily allowed me to touch her, we sat shoulder to shoulder, facing in opposite directions for fifteen minutes. That was all it took for Emily to begin establishing a sense of safety with touch.

There is a reason why this works. Our tissue has its own, powerful memory. When one human's tissue comes into contact with another human's tissue, the tissue begins speaking its own language. That day, Emily's tissue and my tissue had a conversation beyond what we could convey to one another through words alone.

A year later, Emily now comes into my office, takes off her shoes, and jumps up on what I refer to as my touch table. When I ask her if she wants to talk or sit for a few minutes first, Emily's response is always the same: "No, I just want to get on the table."

Because trauma memory is stored in our tissues, on the touch table, I work with my clients' nervous system, which includes the fascia. Fascia is the thin layer of tissue that covers our entire body's musculature. It is here in the fascia that we store the emotions that become stuck in our body. Until we release the fascia, stuck emotions remain stagnant.

In my touch work, I particularly concentrate on the brain stem, where we hold on to our fight and flight responses; the adrenals and kidneys, which moderate stress hormones; and the vagus nerve, which carries signals back and forth between the brain and the gut (often aptly referred to as our "second brain").

Once I begin touching someone's body, they often have the experience of thoughts and memories rising up. This is not a coincidence. The body guides us to what needs to be and is ready to be resolved. Interesting things happen when trauma is released from the body. This can include spontaneous movement, the generation of heat, shaking, and tears. A person's physical reaction depends on what they need to release. This physical release provides a way of working through trauma that doesn't require them to revisit their trauma in the way that talk therapy does.

In addition to touch, this and other types of movement are also a necessary element to bring us back into our body, and that is why it can be so healing. Stored trauma is released through spontaneous movement (the type of movement that happens in therapeutic sessions). With this, we are literally moving the residue of trauma that is stuck within us out so that the trauma can be renegotiated in our system. Additionally, movement in general can make us happy. Have you noticed how children intuitively move their bodies? Or how when you really let loose and dance, it is often accompanied by a sense of freedom and feeling of joy? That is not an accident, and it is why movement therapies are so powerful.

These are the type of breakthroughs that cannot happen in top-down therapy for the simple reason that the element of touch and movement absent.

## THE ROOTS OF BOTTOM-UP THERAPY

Wilhelm Reich, who was part of the same analysis school as Freud, was the father of body-based psychology. His big idea was that muscle tension was the direct result of repressed emotions. He referred to this as body armor, and practiced utilizing pressure to release emotions. It's interesting to look back at that time as a crossroads. Obviously, the vast majority of the Western world turned the corner with Freud, but what if it had been Reich who captured the collective consciousness? As it was, Freud arrived in the United States in 1911 and monopolized the therapeutic world through the late 1970s.

Although Reich was the first psychologist to turn his attention to body-based healing, there was a long tradition of body-mind holistic healing before him. Body-based healing is not a new concept; in fact, it's much older than our Western cognitive approach. In the Eastern traditions, Ayurvedic medicine was practiced as early as 3000 BC. Ayurveda is a holistic system designed to create harmony between the body, mind, and spirituality. The movement medicine of yoga also dates back to this period. Around that same period, we also have our first record of Chinese Medicine, which looks at the body-mind as an energy field. Because of this, you cannot have health in one without health in the other; they go hand in hand.

Greek physician Hippocrates, who lived in the third century BC, was the first person on record to attempt to understand the link between the body, emotions, and healing. He argued that disease is the product of diet, lifestyle, and environmental factors. Ancient Rome adopted this belief and developed public health systems in an attempt to prevent the spread of germs and to maintain holistically healthier populations. In nineteenth-century Europe, there was a movement toward holistic healing and mind-body care.

Reich cracked open the door for much more work to come over the centuries, including that of Peter Levine, who went on to become the founder of Somatic Experiencing therapy. Somatic Experiencing therapy is the end result of Levine asking some important questions, such as, why aren't animals in the wild traumatized by events in the same way domestic animals and human beings are? Levine ultimately came to realize that wild animals have a habit that human beings (and some domestic animals) do not. You have likely seen this behavior yourself, perhaps in your dog. After an animal, for example, escapes being chased down in the wild, it begins to shake. What it is doing is literally shaking the trauma out of its body. The animal is regulating and resetting its nervous system.

Levine noticed that modern civilization works in the exact opposition to this trauma-healing instinct. Let's say you were to get into a car accident. An ambulance would arrive on the scene to take you to the hospital. The first thing the paramedics would tell you is, "Don't move." They would then proceed to strap you down. It is the exact *opposite* of what your nervous system actually needs to do to expunge trauma. Have you ever noticed that you begin to shake or tremble in moments of fear? That is your body, attempting to regulate itself. But in today's world, we don't pay credence to that. We ignore—and even prevent—this very natural reaction of ours. One that, in fact, serves a great purpose.

Levine decided to experiment with this, and he noticed that if he allowed his patients to move through the spontaneous movements that occur in the wake of trauma, they were able to discharge the energy that would otherwise become locked in their body. These movements can take on different forms—for example, shaking, crying, or sweating.

Regardless of what the movement is, it accomplishes the same purpose; it allows the patient to complete an experience in a safe way. Interestingly, this works not only in the immediate aftermath of an event, but also long after an event. The timing is not important (although, obviously, the more quickly a person can resolve trauma, the more freedom they have), but the completion is.

## THE STRUCTURE OF THE BRAIN

Before we can truly understand why it's nothing short of necessary to bring our body into therapeutic settings, it's important to understand how the brain and body are intricately connected.

The brain is composed of three different parts: the reptilian brain, the limbic system, and the neocortex. Each is responsible for different functions.

The reptilian brain is the first part of our brain to develop and its sole purpose is survival. It is where our survival instincts are stored, beginning from the time when we are in utero. It governs our heart rate, breath, nervous system, and perception of our body and the world around us. The reptilian brain has no sense of language or reasoning, and works only according to sensation. It is because of this part of the brain that a baby knows to cry when it is hungry. It feels the sensation and then acts in such a way to promote survival. In other words, the reptilian brain is pure instinct. It is where our fight, flight, or freeze mechanism is triggered, which means that it prompts our body into action.

The reptilian brain also stores our sensory memory from previous experiences. Our experiences are accompanied by sensation memory, and this part of the brain is where they are stored. The reptilian brain works with our tissues in this way. Going back to the phrase "your issues are in your tissues"—our issues live there because our tissues store sensation memory, which our reptilian brain translates into information that can be used for our survival. This is how we make decisions. Yes, our brain is involved, but the process begins with our body.

Our sensory memory is responsible for our impulsive reactions. This explains why my entire childhood came to light in the course of the body scan during the meditation retreat. I was finally able to access the implicit memories stored in my body from my childhood, and to understand why I only felt my body when it was in a state of discomfort. The sensory memory in my reptilian brain meant that I could continue to be comfortably uncomfortable by starving myself and over exercising. I could completely cut off from any sense of feeling my body.

This sensory experience was a way to survive. It was the pain-body that gave me a sense of safety during childhood and, again, as an adult who felt scared in the world and insecure in my attachments. My reptilian brain knew that feeling my body without pain was dangerous. The reptilian brain only knows sensation and repetition. Its purpose is to create homeostasis in the body.

The limbic system—which includes the hypothalamus, amygdala, thalamus, and hippocampus—is higher functioning than the reptilian brain and the second part of our brain to develop in a significant way. It connects the higher- and lower-functioning parts of the brain and regulates our nervous system's response to emotional stimulation. Here we store emotions and memories, and the limbic system also controls functions such as motivation.

Finally, we get to the neocortex, which holds our executive functions. This includes higher-level activities, such as reasoning and logic. This is the part of the brain that separates humans from animals; we are the only species that has a neocortex and, thus, the ability to perform these executive functions.

Our brains continue to develop and come fully online in the several months following birth, while we are preverbal. This means that babies are gathering and storing a ton of information, even before their brains are able to put it all together and use it. You can think of a baby's brain like this: the circuit board has been built, but all of the circuits are not yet hooked up. During this wiring process, the neuropathways babies are utilizing become stronger, while the ones they don't use dwindle. This means that if a baby experiences a chaotic early life, the neurons that are firing to keep them safe will become the strongest and most firmly hooked into the circuit board. It is why children with developmental trauma have a higher incidence of mental health disease as adults; their brains were not built to be as resilient as that of a child without trauma.

## THE NERVOUS SYSTEM

Whenever we are in a state of fear or trauma, our autonomic nervous system, which is associated with the physiology of stress and governs our responses to both internal and external stimuli, kicks into high gear. This system contributes to how we regulate every function in our body, including everything from our breath to our intestines to our bladder.

If we don't resolve trauma or remain in a constant state of fear, our sympathetic nervous system, which is responsible for fight or flight, remains switched on and our bodies suffer the consequences. We were not meant to live this way. The sympathetic branch of our autonomic nervous system is designed for the purposes of switching on in short spurts to energize and mobilize us in those moments when we need to enact our fight or flight reflexes. Because we don't know how to reset our nervous system, many of us today live in a perpetual state of fight and flight.

Again, we come back to this idea of why seeking to address and remedy this state cognitively simply does not work. Our nervous system makes our *bodies* uncomfortable and our bodies respond in kind. That is where we feel the ramifications of our nervous system. We get stuck in some variety of survival mode, whether it's fight, flight, or freeze. And some people feel a combination, almost like they're pressing down on the gas pedal and the brake at the same time.

## THE CONNECTION BETWEEN BRAIN, BODY, AND TRAUMA

We have to pay heed to what our body is telling us so that we can discern the messages and reactions that live within us, and then reanimate the body with a different set of memories. Our reptilian brain, where our sensory memories are stored, triggers our survival instincts. This means that we *must* deal with trauma on a holistic level in order to heal it.

This is why it is so important to see trauma through on a sensory level. That is what gets us "unstuck." It's how we create new instinctual reactions. We must work through the lingering energy of trauma (which presents itself as a sensation) to see it fully through and process it. It is only by seeing these sensations through that our reptilian brain can understand that these sensations are not, in fact, going to kill us. The more we are able to feel these sensations, the more mastery we gain over our embodied experience. We achieve a sense of completion, which allows the trauma energy to be expunged from our body. Once the trauma energy is gone, so is our sense of being endangered or threatened.

It's important to remember that while most trauma occurs within a finite period of time, traumatic memories exist outside of time and space when they are incomplete. Any time we feel a reminiscent sense of danger—whether real or perceived—we go right back to that unfinished trauma business. Our tissues cry out to our reptilian brain and it fires our nervous system into a survival response. If we do not find a way to get rid of that energy, it becomes locked in our body, where it accumulates and impacts the way that we interact with the world and with ourselves.

This need for completion is why talk therapy alone is not enough. Even if our brains can think through how we might have gotten ourselves to safety in the midst of trauma, our tissues and reptilian brain do not speak the same language, so the message is lost in translation.

When a dear friend of mine named Jack was twenty-four, he was driving his girlfriend home one night after studying for the bar exam. After dropping her off, Jack headed home. Along the way, he drove under an elevated train track, which was held up by concrete pillars. As Jack was under the track, a car filled with eight high schoolers cut him off, lost control, and smashed into one of the cement pillars while going eighty miles per hour. Jack slammed on the brakes and was okay but bore witness to eight kids slaughtered on the road before him, including one under the wheel of his car.

Even though Jack wasn't at fault, the law holds that a complicit person cannot leave the scene of the crime and, in this scenario, Jack was considered complicit. He was stuck there for hours amidst screaming, sirens, and an incredibly disturbing clean-up, all of which he had to witness.

After this night, Jack continued moving forward in life. He took the bar exam, got married, and had two kids. Today he is fifty-four and afraid of everything. His kids weren't allowed to eat sushi when they were little. Last summer, he went into a panic that we were all going to get West Nile as we ate dinner outside. Not surprisingly, he is a hypervigilant driver, constantly slamming on the brakes, and distrustful of every other driver on the road. The list of fears goes on and on. He views everything through the lens of danger because he was never able to expunge the trauma energy from his body, so it's just stuck, constantly dysregulating his nervous system and skewing his perception of the world around him. At this point, he has spent an entire half of his life in an arrested state.

Jack's body and reptilian brain are constantly in communication, telling him there is danger around every corner and that he must live in an ongoing fight for survival. I have met so many other people who live their lives in a similar state, and I can tell you this: no matter how big or tragic the trauma, there's no need to keep living with it. It's just a matter of allowing ourselves to see it through to completion.

## HOW OUR BRAIN AND BODY INTERPRET THE WORLD

Here it's important to go back to the idea of how we sense our body and the world.

Interoception is the way in which we sense and feel our body. This applies at the basic level of how we feel temperature, sense that we are being touched, feel pain in our body, feel our heartbeat, and feel how we feel being *in* our body. For example, do we feel sick or do we feel healthy? Do we feel hungry and do we feel safe? Interoception impacts our procedural memory, which is our motor skills and how we do things.

Our sense of interoception is in place from the beginning, and if a baby and primary caregiver have a healthy attachment (in other words, if the caregiver picks up on the baby's cues and addresses them appropriately), then the baby's interoception will continue to develop in a healthy way. For example, if a baby feels the sensation of hunger, cries, and is fed, the baby will continue to feel hunger and express that hunger so that its needs are met. However, if the baby feels hunger and the primary caregiver does not pick up on the cue or address it, the baby will cut themselves off from the hunger so that it can feel safe. As you can see here, there is an element of feedback to the development of healthy and attuned interoception and that feedback is based on social engagement. Our basic sense of safety begins here, with interoception.

Let's expand on this a little bit. People often talk about how they have a high pain tolerance with a certain sense of pride. They might be bleeding and not even realize it. What we translate as a high pain tolerance is actually often a flag for developmental trauma. It's an indicator that a person has cut off their interoception—specifically, their sense of pain—because they were programmed at a young age that the pain would not be properly addressed. They maladapted to not feel the pain so that they could feel safe. It is impossible to feel safe when a basic need is not being met, so it is safer not to feel that pain at all.

This concept doesn't apply only to negative experiences. If we learn that feeling positive feelings such as excitement or joy is not safe, we can also cut our body off from feeling pleasurable sensations. Additionally, our sense of interoception can also be cranked up to high for various reasons, to the point where we are overly sensitive, which can also be unhealthy. Again, this is generally linked back to developmental experiences with our primary caregiver and our need to feel safety within our external environment.

The bottom line is that if our interoception is tweaked, it can lead us to false conclusions. This is how we sense danger when it is not there and when our instincts can lead us astray. Ultimately, it impacts our nervous system and creates emotional dysregulation.

Exteroception is the flip side of interoception; it is how we perceive the outside environment or the world. When we put our hand to someone's forehead to gauge if they have a fever? That is exteroception. The outside environment (the other person) impacts how our hand feels. Exteroception also begins very early on in life and can be impeded by birth and post-birth experiences, as well as by insecure attachments to primary caregivers.

Our exteroception formulates the basis for how we evaluate and assess the world. It feeds into our interoception and what we, in turn, feel about the world.

Proprioception involves how our body replies to time and space. For example, how do we experience our arms in relationship to our legs? This is an important part of our safety system. For example, we want to know that if someone is coming toward us and we need to run, we can get ourselves to safety.

Finally, there is neuroception, the process through which neural circuits distinguish whether people and situations are safe, dangerous, or life-threatening. Our neuroception brings together all of the signals and sensations that our interoception, exteroception, and proprioception are picking up on and sending out. You can think of neuroception as the umbrella that holds the other three modes of perception. The thing is that, as humans, we don't necessarily think of all of these things as perceptions; instead, we think of them as *facts*.

All of these different perceptions involve appropriate communication between our brain, body, and emotions. Since they are constantly working in tandem with one another, if any one of these elements is off, it skews all three. Together, our brain, body, and emotions impact how our nervous system functions, and we can't heal the nervous system without addressing all three of these equally important factors.

## THE ROLE OF EMOTION

It's important to understand how much we impede our perception of the world around us when we disconnect from our bodies. As human beings, our sensory experiences are intricately tied to our emotional experiences. This happens on a basic level: if you are feeling cold not only will you experience sensations around that, but also emotions about being cold. If you have nostalgic memories of cold winter days during your childhood, those emotions might be positive. If, on the other hand, you went through a period of life where you couldn't warm up, you might feel negative emotions.

You can think of emotions as your body's interpretation of a sensation. We think of emotions as existing in our head, and they don't. Consider this for a moment: when you experience anxiety, is it a thought or a feeling in your body?

In a healthy, fully functioning nervous system, we experience the emotions as they are connected to our present situation; however, for many of us who have stressed nervous systems, a sensory experience will trigger an emotion from an earlier point. And when we are unwilling to fully feel our sensations, the emotions associated with them are not processed, which keeps us reliving the past over and over again each time we are triggered by a sensory event.

## DETACHING FROM OUR BODIES

Most of us think of our bodies as a primary element of being human, so at first it can be a strange idea that we would detach from them. How would that even happen? It happens all the time, in ways that we are largely unaware of, and it can happen at any point in our lives for any number of reasons.

Let's take the case of a child who grew up in a house where, for whatever reason, she didn't feel safe. Maybe that sense of safety was the result of abuse, neglect, or even something more mundane like general chaos. That child is going to feel unsafe and failed by their caregiver, whose primary job is to keep them safe. That child will do anything possible to stay attached to that caregiver in hopes of a sense of safety, including giving up their autonomy.

Let's say that this same child is told, "Be a good girl, don't cry." In order to stay in relationship with her primary caregiver, that child will likely give up her own emotional experience when it veers into territory that the caregiver has deemed out of bounds. In order to survive, she begins to believe she can't cry or express her feelings. She can't develop into the person who she naturally is because her caregiver says not to, and that attachment is critical for safety. So, to stay attached to the caregiver, the child detaches from herself. To detach from herself, the child has to detach from her sensory body.

Or let's say that an umbilical cord wraps around an infant's neck during birth, causing them to lose oxygen. This child will never consciously remember that this happened, but the event lives on in their body. Their first experience in the world in their body is not a safe one, so why would that person want to exist within that body?

Take it back even further, and we can even detach from our bodies before birth. Because a mother co-regulates her baby as it is in utero, the baby can sense when its mother is in a state of stress. Not only that, but the stress is passed along to the baby, who will go on to either freeze in overwhelm or replicate the stress (fight or flight).

When we detach from our bodies, we are reacting to fear. We are trying to avoid fear and pain. Fear is a sensory, body-based experience. To avoid fear, we have to avoid our body. This avoidance is just a survival mechanism from our caveman days kicking in. It is a mechanism that was meant to serve us in acute situations, not as a way of life. Until we can feel our pain, we cannot move beyond it. For example, if you happen to suffer from anxiety, but always avoid it, you can never learn to master it—or, at the least, work through it. As a result, you live your life stuck, in a constant state of avoidance and maladaptive behaviors. At least theoretically, I think most of us can agree that it makes far more sense in the long run to feel that anxiety in our body, understand that it won't kill us, and slowly learn to work through it or allow it to reach its climax and dissipate. This is a process, but it's a process that works. And it's a process that has to happen in your body, not in your mind.

## LEARNING A NEW LANGUAGE

Because so many of us have spent so much time living outside of our bodies, when clients come to me, I am essentially teaching them a new language. A while ago, I was running a Somatic Experiencing group. I began our meeting by telling them that we were going to check in, but that I did not want any details about what had happened to them in the past week. Instead, I wanted to know about their felt sense. I explained that we were going to get out of our story and, instead, put words to our experiences. I saw eight pairs of confused eyes looking at me.

"I'll go first," I said. "I had a really big week last week. In the two days leading up to a new, out-of-the-box professional experience, I noticed that I felt a sense of anxiety. I couldn't sit still for very long, and I kept finding myself doing X, Y, and Z. Then, as I got into the thick of the experience, I noticed that my anxiety turned into excitement, and I was able to experience a sense of mastery."

When we connect with our experience rather than our story, we can begin to move toward a more embodied way of dealing with our trauma. But before we can begin to do this, we have to begin to build the ability to feel and articulate our experiences, because trauma often impedes our ability to even know what we are experiencing.

Because body-based psychology necessitates people to

both listen to, sit with, and move with their bodies—the very thing they have been avoiding—there is certainly some discomfort required. As a therapist, it is my job to teach clients how to begin to tolerate this discomfort. Building up this tolerance usually begins in my office, and then extends to the outside world. It can be small things, like being able to withstand the physical reaction your body feels to telling a friend "no" when you know they want you to say "yes." But once you can do this, you can connect in a way that feels more fluid, less stressful, and more authentic.

I often hear some variation of this statement from my clients: "I'm so uncomfortable. What do I do?"

And I tell them, "How about just noticing that you're uncomfortable, that the discomfort is causing you pain, and you don't want to be experiencing this?"

In this simple action, you come online as your own observer. You are taken out of the cognitive exercise of asking *why* you feel uncomfortable, and instead come online in your body, in the moment, with what is happening now. You don't avoid. Instead, you learn that the pain won't kill you. Instead, you learn to make peace with and lean into the discomfort.

Of course, this is easier said than done. Clients tell me all the time that sitting in that state, with that discomfort, is too hard or that they don't even know how to. I get that. But learning how to sit with ourselves, how to become our own observer, is nonetheless the first step toward healing from the bottom up.

CHAPTER THREE

———

# TRAUMA: WE'VE ALL GOT IT

While some psychological conditions, such as schizophrenia, are certainly the result of chemical imbalances, in my experience the vast majority of psychological and mental health issues stem from trauma. And, as you now know, trauma lives within the body, not the brain. This means that trauma, without exception, cannot be healed simply by changing your thoughts and behaviors. It has to be healed in the place where it lives—in the body. Anything else will only act as a Band-Aid and will fail to address the underbelly of what is causing a person to feel, react, and interact the way they do.

You've probably noticed that I have already used the word trauma several times throughout the course of this book. Trauma is one of those words that has been stigmatized.

We often think of people who have been through trauma as somehow broken or victimized. The truth of the matter is that every human being has at some point been traumatized, whether they recognize it as such or not. Yes, that includes you.

We tend to think of trauma as a rare, extenuating circumstance. But the fact of the matter is that, whether we remember it or not, most of us have experienced trauma in our lives. Of course, trauma can come through random occurrences such as a car accident or assault. But it can also happen in more day-to-day or situational circumstances. We can even be traumatized as the result of events that we don't consciously remember. That is, our brains might not remember the trauma; our bodies do.

Trauma is not about an event. As Peter Levine explains it, trauma is the result of the energy that gets locked in our body when it experiences threats, both real and perceived. When trauma energy becomes trapped, the body interprets it as a survival mechanism. For example, if your nervous system freezes in response to trauma, you can get locked into a freeze state, which will re-emerge every time something triggers a sense of danger. Same with fight and flight. Energy becomes trapped when we are unable to see a traumatic event through to completion. In other words, trauma occurs when we lose our sense of safety and it is only resolved when the body is restored to a sense of safety. For example, if you find yourself in a situation in which you want to run for safety but for whatever reason are unable to, you can get locked into that flight mode until you somehow resolve that incident to completion later down the line.

This locking in happens because when we are under threat, our body creates a massive amount of energy for the purposes of self-defense. When that energy is not discharged, our autonomic nervous system loses its capacity to restore equilibrium. *It's important to understand that this energy does not dispel on its own accord over time.* It will continue to live on within us until we address it by completing our self-protective responses. That is, in a nutshell, the biology of healing.

The truth of the matter is that there can never be one standard description of or marker for trauma, because everyone experiences it differently. Ten people might go through the exact same experience, but each person will interpret it differently, not only mentally and emotionally, but also physically. The sooner a person can restore their sense of safety, the sooner the trauma is resolved. It's the same as when two people have a conversation but describe it in two totally different ways and walk away with two totally different interpretations. Each of us has our own way of perceiving the world and our experience in it. Some people are more easily traumatized than others. Some people have an easier time expunging trauma than others. Our perception and experience of trauma are largely determined by three factors: genetics, previous trauma, and how safe we generally feel in the world. How safe we feel in the aftermath of a potentially traumatizing event also comes into play here.

## DEVELOPMENTAL TRAUMA

Within trauma, there are several categories, including developmental trauma, complex trauma, acute trauma, multigenerational trauma, and collective trauma. Developmental trauma includes any traumatic events or situations that occur during one's developmental years. This span of time ranges all the way from in utero through the pre-verbal years and up to age three. A child can be traumatized when a mother is ill or experiences depression or anxiety while the child is in the womb, because it secretes hormones into the unborn baby that change its chemical balance. The more stress hormones a baby acquires, the more that child's body will prepare for threat. Not only that, but it can create a whole host of issues, ranging from allergies and asthma to learning challenges.

Developmental trauma can also occur as a result of a singular incident, such as if the pregnant mother is in a car accident. The impact of this sort of scenario is dependent upon how regulated the mother's nervous system is.

Does her heart rate stay up for the next three months or does she quickly rebalance? Does she experience stress every time she gets in the car from that point forward, or does she resume life as normal? Based on these factors, an event like this can have an entire range of effects on an unborn child, running the gamut from severe to non-existent.

Even something as simple as a vaginal birth can be regulating to a baby's nervous system as it pushes off of the uterine walls. An emergency C-section might create stress in a baby's body, which can register as traumatic. There are so many seemingly innocuous ways in which a young child can be traumatized. Ways that the child will never consciously remember and that their parents will never even be aware of.

Someone who has experienced developmental trauma may have never had—or, at least, may not remember— ever having felt a sense of safety in the world or within themselves. They don't have that as a touchstone or barometer for how life *could* potentially feel. I notice that many of my clients who have developmental trauma are always waiting for something bad to happen. Resolving this requires a process of moving that person toward a place where they can build a sense of safety within themselves. It is a layered process and that process begins with building a new, stable foundation. That foundation generally begins by building a safe cocoon within the therapist-client relationship.

Here's an example of what building a safe place to deal with developmental trauma might look like with a bottom-up approach. I have a nineteen-year-old client who is eating disordered and an overachiever. She recently came in and told me that she had been suffering from a two-day panic attack. Rather than asking this woman what triggered the panic attack (as a top-down therapeutic approach would), I asked her, "What is happening for you right now?"

"I feel like I just want to get into the fetal position," she replied.

"Great!" I replied. "Let's do that."

I bunkered this woman in with pillows, creating a cocoon for her. She spent the next hour encased in those pillows in the fetal position as I sat next to her and gently put my hands on her feet. By the time she left the session, she was amazed that she was able to quiet her mind and felt far more grounded than she had when she first walked through the door. She learned that she could stay *in* her body in those moments of panic and it was going to be okay—better, even! This provided her with a new sense of mastery.

If this sounds simple, that's because it was. All I did was to create a safe container for this young woman to move through an experience. Of note here is the fact that this woman knew exactly what her body needed, whether she was aware of it before coming to my office or not. All I had to do was ask.

We don't need to know what happened with this woman to traumatize her or to trigger that trauma. The story doesn't matter, because we're not working with it and would likely never be able to understand what that story is, anyway. That is not how this issue is going to be resolved. It is going to be resolved through her body and through her nervous system, which is at the root of these panic attacks. So the extent of our talking was limited to that simple question and her answer to it: What is happening and what do you need?

You can probably see how it becomes difficult to work through these issues of developmental trauma in talk therapy. How can a person possibly get to the root of their trauma if they cannot even remember the incident that led them to this place?

Developmental trauma is always less about the specifics of what happened and more about the person's reaction to it. If something causes a person to squelch their feelings or behave in such a way that their basic needs are not met, it is likely unresolved trauma.

## PTSD AND COMPLEX PTSD

You may already be familiar with PTSD and its impact on war veterans and survivors of severe accidents and other acute events. The causes of PTSD might also include events such as surgeries or medical issues, surviving a natural disaster, or something seemingly far more mundane than any of these things. The trauma might be physical, or it might be emotional or mental. The similarity between all of these traumas is that they leave a person feeling unsafe and with a sense of loss or disconnection to themselves and the world they live in.

Complex PTSD is different from this more commonly recognized form of acute PTSD in that it is the result of cumulative trauma acquired through chronic or long-term exposure to stress, which most often occurs during childhood. In other words, complex PTSD is not attached to a single event.

Complex PTSD develops when a child doesn't feel safe over and over again or does not have a secure attachment to their primary caregiver. There is the sense that their physical or mental well-being is being compromised. It might involve abuse, neglect, chaos, or being immersed in a pervasive environment of stress. This type of trauma impacts a child on an ongoing basis in a similar way that developmental trauma does. It can cause an individual to live in a constant state of fear when no fear is present.

Like developmental trauma, it can completely alter a person's perception of the world.

## COLLECTIVE TRAUMA AND MULTIGENERATION TRAUMA

Collective trauma is when an entire community identifies with a story about or event from the past. As a result, there exists a universal overwhelming sense of fear, disconnection with other communities, or sense of helplessness. It is very difficult to move forward and create repair when everyone exists within this same state. Collective trauma can also self-perpetuate in the children who are born into those communities. This might happen as the result of instances such as natural disaster, war, terrorism, or even pervasive poverty or high crime rates.

Multi-generational trauma can also fall under the category of collective trauma. As we are developing, we need our primary caregiver to co-regulate us. When they are unable to do so because of their inability to resolve their own trauma—or the symptoms of that trauma—trauma can be inherited, so to speak. For example, if an infant is raised by someone who exists in a high state of anxiety, that anxiety will become the child's inheritance. The nervous system chemically changes and produces more stress hormones when we exist in a stressful environment. If a child is raised in this sort of atmosphere, their nervous system will maladapt to it. We've learned a lot about this through the study of epigenetics, and particularly through the study of the descendants of Holocaust survivors. Even though the second-generation of Holocaust survivors did not experience direct trauma, they are still impacted because of how the first generation shows up in their lives and the impact they have on the co-regulation of the second-generation's nervous system.

## THE IMPACT OF TRAUMA

The root of one's trauma is less important than how it impacts their life down the line. Many people get stuck in what the Somatic Experiencing community calls a trauma vortex; this is when people begin to live in an ongoing state dictated by damage that has been done in the past. The trauma vortex is where and why the nervous system is most dysregulated, because the trauma story is activated here and the stress hormones are constantly pumping as a result. It is when we are in this state that physical symptoms begin to manifest themselves. We cannot achieve a true state of homeostasis while in the trauma vortex, because our nervous system is constantly sensing danger, even when it is not present. In the trauma vortex, we are living with all of our survival defense mechanisms switched on.

I worked with a client named Amy who personifies how

painful the trauma vortex can be to exist in. Amy grew up in a household that was ruled by physical and emotional abuse. She constantly talked about how awful life was and how depressed she felt. As Amy viewed it, there was nowhere safe in the world, and no sense of joy or happiness to be found. She was able to find a problem with every potential bright spot or solution in her life, and this viewpoint extended to how she saw herself, as well—just like everything else in the world, she was never good or right. Amy simply could not see what a powerful and capable human being she actually was.

The trauma vortex looks a little bit different for everyone, but for Amy it meant that she couldn't see the forest through the trees. Even when things were going well, she couldn't trust it because the feeling of safety was just too uncomfortable and unfamiliar. During her childhood, Amy had become accustomed to the notion that the other shoe was always about to drop. As a child, Amy was not safe, and as an adult, she didn't trust that she had the capacity to be in charge of her own ability to feel safe.

It is impossible to heal when we are stuck in the trauma vortex like Amy was. Healing requires getting out of this black hole so that we can establish skills such as resilience and obliterate stories about victimhood. We will never find a sense of safety and attunement with self in the trauma vortex, nor can we begin to re-enter the present moment. Achieving this requires pulling out of the aftermath of trauma and the accompanying sense of helplessness or a lack of safety.

People get stuck in a trauma vortex because of the unresolved trauma energy that is locked in the body. It impacts everything: how someone moves through the world, sees the world, and senses danger. It impacts their sense of the behavior of others, how they are being treated, and their response to interactions with others. It affects their sense of autonomy and ability to have a fully embodied life experience.

These are the things we need to address when we think about the impact of trauma. Each and every one of these issues has an adverse impact on our relationships and experience of the world on a day-to-day basis.

Because most people who have been traumatized are disconnected from themselves, it is incredibly difficult to form deeper, more meaningful, and more authentic attachments and relationships to others. If we cannot feel safe within ourselves, how can we possibly feel safe with others? For some people, this looks like the inability to attach to others. They isolate because they cannot find a sense of trust or safety in their relationships. Other people overly attach. That attachment feels so important and so vital to their safety and survival that they may very well feel safer giving up their relationship with themselves than their relationship with the other person. Learning to build healthy, safe attachments is critical because human beings are wired for connection. This experience of safe attachment begins in the therapeutic relationship as the therapist teaches the client to learn to attach to themselves.

My goal is to help my clients learn to feel safe enough to trust their inner voice. Once they trust that voice, their behavior can follow. This is how a person changes their relationship to themselves. It's how they begin to move through the world with a sense of secure attachment with themselves, and *this* allows them to be in real relationships with others.

Let's take a look at how trauma manifests in practice and how we can move through it in a body-centric way.

### FIGHTING THE FREEZE

Kim was a well-adjusted, outgoing, social college student. Then, one night, as she was walking home from a party, she was attacked and raped at knifepoint. Kim instinctually knew that if she fought back, she would put herself in grave danger, so she didn't.

For the next few weeks, Kim was more than understandably a bit shaken up but, from the outside, she appeared to bounce back from the assault incredibly well. She graduated from college and went on to work at a publishing house. The environment was stressful but, still, everything seemed fine. Kim managed her deadlines and appeared to deal with stress in a healthy way.

Then, about two years into the job, Kim noticed that she was feeling more and more anxious, to the point where she became paralyzed and couldn't finish anything she started, including her work. It was almost as if she went into a freeze state. Interestingly, Kim only began experiencing this when a new, strong-minded male boss was hired. After a while, Kim also started to notice that she began to lose her words whenever she was around him. As more time went by, Kim began losing her ability to articulate around *all* men. Whereas she had once been confident, she now often questioned herself.

Around the same time Kim's new boss started, she also got into a new relationship. The closer she got to her boyfriend, the more trouble she had articulating her feelings to him. She felt uncomfortable asking for what she needed so, often, didn't ask at all. Whenever Kim found herself wanting something she couldn't ask for, she felt her muscles tense up.

After a while, it all caught up with Kim. Her anxiety

continued to ramp up to the point where she couldn't hold it together. She quit her job, began avoiding social situations, and eventually found herself sabotaging her relationship.

Kim finally reached a point where she realized she needed help, and it was then that she came to see me. It was evident that, as a result of the assault, Kim had become locked in a freeze state. Our work was to practice moving Kim out of these freeze states in a non-threatening way. This involved reconnecting and reattaching Kim with her body, and sensory experience in a way that felt comfortable to her.

Once Kim was able to do this, things began to shift. The only way we can undo trauma is to re-experience the survival mechanism and move beyond it. In Kim's case, that meant I had to help her visualize safely moving through the assault so that she could have a physical experience of what it would be like to defend herself.

Kim is an interesting study because, like so many of us, she was able to keep the impact of her trauma contained for a long time. To the point where everyone—including Kim—assumed she had fully recovered and was fine. It wasn't until Kim became closely connected to male figures (like her assailant) that her body came back into that same defensive posture it had been in during the knife attack. It was then that the unresolved trauma came rushing forward and Kim automatically went back to her default survival mechanism—the freeze.

It's important to note that the male figures in Kim's life who triggered her were not a threat—neither Kim's boss nor her boyfriend were problematic or posed any sort of threat. The problem is that Kim sensed danger where it was not present because this is what happens when there is an incomplete survival response. The experience becomes lost in the body and the person returns to that default survival skill when stress and tension increase. Because Kim had not resolved the trauma of her past, she sensed danger in the present and reacted accordingly.

Kim is not unusual. In fact, I see a lot of cases in which people's trauma responses creep up on them later on down the line. Stress tends to bring up trauma responses, as does attachment (which is why Kim's boyfriend was triggering). Many traumatized people find that the more strongly they attach to a person, the more there is to lose, and if that attachment feels insecure, they begin to feel threatened. This happens a lot, although it's not always easy to recognize. Have you ever noticed that most relationships are blissful until about six months to a year in, when things start to go sideways? This is because it is around this point when people tend to attach and connect to their partners more deeply. If there is trauma or a breach in attachment in a person's past, their nervous system begins to fire.

## STOPPING THE FIGHT

Jake is a veteran who returned overseas after being injured in a car bomb explosion. At the time of the blast, Jake was with another soldier who fled the scene, leaving Jake to fend for himself. Jake tried to run, but his injuries kept him stuck in the line of fire. His instinctual survival mechanism was thwarted based on circumstance.

For the first six months or so after returning home, Jake felt swathed in a metaphorical pink cloud. He felt safe and life felt good again. Then, after those initial months, Jake began to settle back into real life. He started interviewing for jobs and, around the time, began to have flashbacks of the bombing. Jake always emerged from these flashbacks angry—he was angry about his injury and angry at the soldier who had left him behind.

More and more, Jake found himself ruminating about the accident, replaying the situation over and over again in his head. Sometimes, he pretended that he had been the soldier to escape unharmed. He began having revenge fantasies about the soldier who had abandoned him. Coincidentally, the other soldier started to call Jake a lot during that time. When they spoke, Jake would unleash on him. Jake told his fellow soldier what a horrible human being he was for leaving him alone. He lost it on this guy. This was the first sign that Jake's nervous system was activated.

From there, things got more intense. Jake began to perceive threats that were not there. His response was to fight, even when people were trying to help him—and people frequently tried to help Jake because of his injury. He didn't trust anyone. If he heard a strange noise on the street, Jake would run in the other direction. He got to the point where he was even triggered by seemingly mundane things, like another person standing too close. Despite himself, Jake started to become verbally abusive to his wife and agitated by any sound his two children made while they were playing. He felt especially volatile when his son played with his toy army trucks.

Clearly, Jake's survival response was to fight despite how misdirected this response was. As time went by, this instinct only became stronger.

Finally, Jake realized that he needed help, and that's when he found me. When Jake and I first met, he didn't trust anyone, so he was understandably apprehensive about me. I believe the only reason he was able to trust me enough to even come in was because he had been referred by a buddy of his who had a lot of anger management issues.

When I first met Jake, the stiffness and rigidity in his body were evident even in the way he held himself. It was obvious that he had a ton of built-up fight energy that needed to be expunged. Especially at the beginning of our sessions, I was very careful to make sure Jake did not re-tell his story because it was so activating and just made the fight energy that much stronger.

We set to work deactivating Jake's nervous system. A large part of this involved building trust. Jake and I talked a lot about his children, who he loved so much despite how they agitated them. "Did you do anything with your kids this weekend?" I might ask. Even in those simple conversations, there was room for Jake and I to not only build trust, but also start to address his nervous system. Jake still had the capacity to have glimpses of connection with his kids, so we would often dive into what it felt like in those moments when he felt joy with his children. This is how we began to show Jake's nervous system that it had the capacity to move out of the trauma vortex and toward the healing vortex.

One step at a time, we worked together to bring Jake back online so that he could reconnect with himself and those tiny moments of joy and levity. From there, we got to the point where we were able to talk about the good things about Jake's time in the military. Eventually, we were able to discuss the bombing and, when he was able to tolerate it from a sensory point of view, we worked our way to Jake's unsuccessful fight response.

We realized that Jake was experiencing a lot of spontaneous movement in his legs. Eventually, Jake allowed me to do some touch work on him as we worked our way through his accident. He learned to tolerate the sensations in his body that arose as we worked through the trauma, and then Jake got to a point where he was able to relax and be more present. Presence is an important key to healing because trauma causes a person to lose all sense of space and time. It removes a person from the here and now and keeps them stuck in and reacting to that moment of traumatization. In other words, a person remains perpetually in danger. By bringing himself into the present moment, Jake's fight response began to melt away.

It was a slow process, but completely transformative for Jake. Today, he is able to work again and, while his fight response has vastly diminished, sometimes he still sees glimpses of it. Jake continues to actively work on calming his system when he is triggered, but he can now tolerate the agitation in his system without becoming overwhelmed. We continue to work together every once and a while, and I am thrilled to say that Jake no longer looks at the world and people around him as a threat. Even in those now-rare moments when he does feel threatened, Jake can slow things down and tolerate that sensory experience in his body. He understands how to check in with himself and can look at the world with a more objective experience.

## WHY TRAUMA ISN'T RESOLVED THROUGH TALK THERAPY

There are two primary issues that make it impossible to resolve trauma through talk therapy or any other sort of cognitive process. The first is that we use cognitive processes to protect and prevent ourselves from experiencing embodied sensory experiences. Remember interception, the way in which our body perceives the world around it? When we bring our mind in to interpret traumatic events, it often creates cognitive dissonance around what our body is telling us. It detaches us from our interception.

Here's what that cognitive dissonance might look like. Let's say a person was assaulted in a dark alley. In talk therapy, they dealt with their ongoing fear of being alone in the dark by telling themselves, "You are safe now. The fear is in your mind." No matter how much they tell themselves this, it still doesn't *feel* safe in those moments when they are walking around alone at night and become triggered. It doesn't prevent their body from experiencing the sensations of fear, however it might prevent the person from allowing themselves to experience that fear in their body by detaching. It certainly prevents them from expunging the trauma energy. Instead, they are trying to override it, which, as you know by now, doesn't work. No matter how much we try to detach or cognitively override a feeling, our emotions and embodied sensations can't be rationalized away. All this accomplishes is blocking us from moving through the experience and expunging the energy.

Another common avoidance tactic is denial. "Oh, I'm *fine*. Everything is great!" They tell themselves this despite all of the messages their body is trying to convey in order to allow the healing process to occur.

Denial is a self-protective mechanism that might buy people a little bit of time before they have to deal with the underlying issue. But one way or another, the reactions will continue to show up in the body until they become unavoidable or cause a person's quality of life to significantly diminish. Sometimes emotions manifest in the form of physical illness, such as an autoimmune disease. I have seen this several times, and one particular client comes to mind.

I work with a super successful African American female client who became pregnant after dating her Asian boyfriend for just a short time. Twenty years later, they are married and have four kids together. They have made it this long despite the fact that this woman cheated on her husband before they even got married, although he didn't find out until later on. By this point, their second child was on the way.

This husband has spent the vast majority of the marriage punishing his wife. He constantly brings up her transgressions and is very critical of everything she does. As a result, my client has never really used her voice in the marriage. She has spent all of this time unhappy, although no one would ever know it from the outside. She just smiles through it all and tries to ignore it, meanwhile experiencing enormous amounts of emotional pain. Things reached a head about five years ago, when her husband became more critical than ever before. Not surprisingly, right around this same point, my client developed vitiligo—an autoimmune disease in which the pigmentation of the skin attacks itself and creates blotchy white spots. I believe it was this woman's body translating the message she got from her husband on a constant basis: "If you were somebody else, I would love you."

This is a prime example of how denial doesn't work. Although my client was imperfect in her relationship, she *wanted* connection. She wanted her husband to love her and she wanted to feel worthy. But she convinced herself not to listen to her sadness, discontent, or ongoing feelings of inferiority. She went into denial.

Our brains can do that...but our bodies cannot.

## TRAUMA SENSITIVITY SCALE

This survey will help you understand how much your daily life is currently affected by trauma. Below is a list of statements about various trauma symptoms you may experience. Please mark how often you experience each symptom.

There are no right or wrong answers, and every person's experience will be unique. It is neither better nor worse if you have a high or low score. What is important is learning more about your mental and emotional health. If at any point in taking this survey you begin to feel uncomfortable, please take a break and come back when you are feeling better.

This survey is also available online at movingbeyondtrauma.co.

1. When something bad happens to me, I have the urge to run away, fight, or feel paralyzed (as if I can't do anything).
   a. Always
   b. Often
   c. Sometimes
   d. Rarely
   e. Never
2. I drift off in conversation and cannot track what is being

said to me or feel as if I am watching myself from the outside looking in.

a. Always

b. Often

c. Sometimes

d. Rarely

e. Never

3. I have unwanted and unpleasant thoughts, memories, pictures, or dreams of past events in my mind.

a. Always

b. Often

c. Sometimes

d. Rarely

e. Never

4. Physical, emotional, or sexual intimacy with a loved one feels uncomfortable.

a. Always

b. Often

c. Sometimes

d. Rarely

e. Never

5. I feel nothing, like I am dead inside or just going through the motions at work or at home.

a. Always

b. Often

c. Sometimes

d. Rarely

e. Never

6. I find myself feeling unsafe for no apparent reason.
    a. Always
    b. Often
    c. Sometimes
    d. Rarely
    e. Never
7. I have a hard time relating to others or feel like I don't fit in.
    a. Always
    b. Often
    c. Sometimes
    d. Rarely
    e. Never
8. I feel restless, dissatisfied, or uncomfortable.
    a. Always
    b. Often
    c. Sometimes
    d. Rarely
    e. Never
9. I have a hard time expressing my needs and/or my inner voice doesn't match my behaviors.
    a. Always
    b. Often
    c. Sometimes
    d. Rarely
    e. Never
10. I worry about the past or the future.
    a. Always

b. Often

c. Sometimes

d. Rarely

e. Never

11. I feel unmotivated, lethargic, and do not enjoy everyday activities.

    a. Always

    b. Often

    c. Sometimes

    d. Rarely

    e. Never

12. I feel people are dangerous or untrustworthy, and I cannot let my guard down around others.

    a. Always

    b. Often

    c. Sometimes

    d. Rarely

    e. Never

13. When I am stressed or upset, I drink alcohol, take drugs, gamble, spend extra money, or take other dangerous risks that I don't when I'm feeling okay.

    a. Always

    b. Often

    c. Sometimes

    d. Rarely

    e. Never

14. I get very stressed under pressure, have a hard time bouncing back, or am easily discouraged when I fail.

a. Always

b. Often

c. Sometimes

d. Rarely

e. Never

15. My inner dialogue says that something is wrong with me, I am no good, or that I am worthless.

a. Always

b. Often

c. Sometimes

d. Rarely

e. Never

16. I tend to avoid people, places, and situations that might trigger me.

a. Always

b. Often

c. Sometimes

d. Rarely

e. Never

17. I find that my emotional reaction can be inappropriate for the situation at hand. For example, I overreact or show no reaction compared to how others would respond.

a. Always

b. Often

c. Sometimes

d. Rarely

e. Never

18. I have a hard time following directions or paying atten-

tion to what people are saying to me.

a. Always

b. Often

c. Sometimes

d. Rarely

e. Never

19. When I make a mistake, I obsess over what I could have done differently or have a very hard time letting it go.

a. Always

b. Often

c. Sometimes

d. Rarely

e. Never

20. I feel the urge to harm myself, especially in an attempt to feel something or to numb out my feelings.

a. Always

b. Often

c. Sometimes

d. Rarely

e. Never

21. I tend to overeat, under eat, or binge and purge.

a. Always

b. Often

c. Sometimes

d. Rarely

e. Never

22. I misinterpret what others are saying or jump to conclusions too quickly.

a. Always

b. Often

c. Sometimes

d. Rarely

e. Never

23. I have trouble falling or staying asleep, or I sleep more than nine hours per night.

a. Always

b. Often

c. Sometimes

d. Rarely

e. Never

24. My emotions feel out of control, I am ashamed of my emotions, or I have emotional outbursts.

a. Always

b. Often

c. Sometimes

d. Rarely

e. Never

25. I feel uncomfortable when someone is chewing too loudly, sucking their teeth, or fidgeting with an object such as keys or a pen.

a. Always

b. Often

c. Sometimes

d. Rarely

e. Never

## CALCULATE YOUR SCORE

Following are instructions for calculating and interpreting your score. Please remember that your score is not a reflection of your worthiness. There are no good or bad scores, and everybody can be helped, no matter what degree of traumatization is present. What matters most is what you do with your score and how motivated you are to make changes in your life.

Please count the number of answers you have for each letter and record it next to the corresponding letter. Next, multiply the count for each letter by its number of points. Finally, add up each subtotal to calculate your final score.

A _____ x 5 = _____

B _____ x 4 = _____

C _____ x 3 = _____

D _____ x 2 = _____

E _____ x 1 = _____

TOTAL = _____

### 106-125 = Very High Trauma Symptoms

You have a very high level of trauma symptoms at this time. This might mean you experienced a lot of traumatic events in your past, had a difficult childhood, or that you react more strongly to traumatic experiences. Remember, this score has no bearing on your ability to heal, and is only a reflection of this current moment. Imagine your healing work moving at a turtle's pace; slow and steady wins the race. The benefit of being a turtle is that you carry your home with you everywhere you go, so there's always a place to take a nap! Moving at this speed means you'll get to enjoy the scenery as you move along your healing journey, get to know parts of yourself you've lost along the way, and emerge with a new relationship with yourself and the world around you.

### 86-100 = High Trauma Symptoms

You presently have a high level of trauma symptoms in your body, though you also have some degree of resilience, or the ability to recover. Your healing work will expand this skill as you learn how to center yourself and feel safe. Imagine yourself moving at the speed of a domestic cat. You can take off in a sprint once in a while, but you generally prefer to meander around. Don't forget to reward yourself along the way with a treat or two.

### 66-85 = Medium Trauma Symptoms

You have a medium level of trauma symptoms, as well as a fair level of nervous system health. Your trauma history might be more sporadic, less severe, or you may have a stronger base to work from than others. Visualize your recovery as though you're a golden retriever on a walk; a well-behaved golden retriever that keeps an even pace, and doesn't pull on the leash or jump on passersby. Take care of yourself throughout this healing process and, in time, you'll be in even better shape, teaching that old dog some new tricks.

## 46-65 = Low Trauma Symptoms

You have a low level of trauma symptoms and your nervous system is reasonably healthy. You have likely had some traumatic experiences in the past, though you have also likely had many positive times that have helped you build a sense of safety in your body. You will be able to move through this work at a horse's pace, fairly quickly, though remember: you're not trying to win a race. Healing means learning to tune in and pay attention to your needs, whether that means going for a gallop, or taking a break to munch on some hay.

## 25-45 = Very Low Trauma Symptoms

You presently have a very low level of trauma symptoms. While you have experienced some degree of trauma, your resilience has helped you get through. You only have minimal effects remaining or issues in just a few areas. Do not negate your discomforts, however; you deserve complete nervous system health. Your healing will move at a cheetah's pace. Like all cats, you still need plenty of cat naps along the way, but you'll likely arrive at your destination sooner than most.

# CHAPTER FOUR

---

# WHAT HEALING LOOKS LIKE

With this understanding of how our brain and body work together, what trauma is, and how it impacts our daily life, let's now turn our attention to what body-based healing looks like in practice. In this chapter, I will share a few of my favorite stories about clients who have found healing from some of the issues that talk therapy struggles to get to the heart of.

While each person's scenario is unique, there do tend to be some underlying themes and commonalities in the issues that follow. It is my hope that you will see through these examples that, no matter where you are today, there is always hope and the very real possibility for a more fulfilling, more vibrant, and richer life experience. It is also my intent to give you insight into what body-based psychology looks like in practice, how it helps to heal, and how it is uniquely catered to the client at hand in a way that top-down therapy simply cannot be.

## HEALING FROM DEPRESSION

Kathy was about fifty years old when I first met with her. She experienced a lot of stress from the time she was in utero and throughout her childhood, which was filled with abuse and neglect. Understandably, Kathy couldn't wait to get out of her childhood home so, at a young age, she married a man who, not surprisingly, turned out to be abusive. After many years, Kathy had the courage and strength to leave the relationship.

Because Kathy spent her entire childhood and early adult life in survival mode, circumnavigating abuse, she never had the opportunity to develop a relationship with herself, or to understand what she needed emotionally. When I met Kathy, her life was dominated by stress. All she could see around her was danger, and she couldn't even identify the safe places that may have existed. She saw what was wrong rather than what was right. This is what stress physiology does, and is a common result of constantly living in survival mode. People like Kathy become adept at identifying danger because they have to; picking up on safety queues is far more difficult and unnatural.

There are other results of a nervous system in distress, too. For example, Kathy did not know how to socially engage, which meant that she was largely isolated. Also, her digestive system was a mess.

Over time, Kathy developed depression as a cumulative response to exhaustion from constantly living life on high alert. Here's the good news: it didn't take me too long into my work with Kathy to realize that she actually *did* have a lot of safe spaces in her life. Her children, then in their early twenties, were functional and safe. But Kathy couldn't even see this—all she was able to see through her lens were the things her children weren't doing at any given point in time. Our work was to allow Kathy to see the world, and all of the safe spaces in it, through new eyes.

## THE TREATMENT

Education was an important first step for Kathy. She had to come to the understanding that nothing that had happened in her life was her fault. Abuse, chaos, and danger were all she had ever known, so of course she didn't have the capacity to trust or feel safe. I have found that, in therapeutic environments, education often has the effect of making clients feel understood, and this was definitely the case with Kathy. It helped her to understand that she wasn't alone, which provided a sense of connection. This was a new feeling for her.

Of course, our main work was in calming down Kathy's stress physiology so that she could learn to accurately assess safety and danger queues. I quickly learned that Kathy did not have a baseline for understanding how to feel joy; she was only versed in sadness, heaviness, and depression.

The first thing we had to do was to help Kathy feel safe enough to experience a sense of joy. When Kathy had these small moments of joy, I made sure to point them out to her so that she could recognize she had the capacity for positive emotions. I made a point of using a lot of humor in our sessions as I introduced her to touch work. One of the things that amazed me about Kathy is the fact that, even though she hadn't had a lot of experiences with safe touch, it was almost as if her body was craving physical connection. I was surprised that she hopped up onto the table almost immediately. When I initially touched her, it felt almost as if her body collapsed.

As a somatic therapist, one of the first areas to address in a client is the hypothalamic pituitary adrenal axis, or the HPA axis. If we can slow the adrenals, the amount of stress hormones pumping through the body decreases. I did this, laying my hands on her adrenals and kidneys, and Kathy began to cry. It was almost as if her tissues were pleading to please give them relief and help them to feel safe. A lot of heat began radiating from her body and, interestingly, early memories of her mom started to drift to the surface. Kathy remembered a moment when she was just three or four years old, alone with her mom, who was crying and holding her as they rocked back and forth. It was almost as if Kathy's mom had been using her to co-regulate for a sense of safety. Rather than Kathy's mom making her child feel safe, the tables were turned. As this came to the surface, Kathy spontaneously started rocking on the table.

In the course of our sessions, Kathy experienced a lot of spontaneous movement and many memories came up for her, which allowed Kathy to cry and mourn them. This spontaneous movement serves a purpose: it allows people who have been traumatized to renegotiate their biological state, and the completion of trauma begins to settle in. Kathy expressed that she wanted to rock, and I helped her do that. It was almost as if Kathy was going back to that movement with her mom, only this time she was being comforted rather than having to fill the role of comforter. With this understanding of Kathy's past, it was clear how she had ended up in an abusive relationship. If a person doesn't experience a healthy attachment with their caregiver, how can they have any sense of accuracy in sensing safety and danger in their relationships later on down the line? We gravitate either toward what's familiar to us or what we have been conditioned to believe. Our system seeks a sense of familiarity.

Kathy and I worked with sensory experiences. One week, I had her go to a department store and pick out perfume samples that she liked. We did many things like this to build what I called a sensory toolbox, some go-to items Kathy could use to bring herself back down and connect when she needed. Kathy sat outside on her back patio, a place that she loved, and I had her create a playlist of songs that moved her so that she could close her eyes and listen to a few songs out there every day, simultaneously calling upon multiple senses. Each week, Kathy had a different assignment. For as much as Kathy was making progress, I couldn't push her back into her body, and these sensory items were able to accomplish that in a non-threatening way.

I did a lot of work on Kathy's brain stem, which is where fight or flight resides; it also serves as the medium between the body and brain communication. I worked to bring more circulation back in there and, all of a sudden, Kathy was able to mobilize without fear. We also did a lot of breath exercises, which regulates heart rate variability and also the vagus nerve when we are in parasympathetic shut down. Today, Kathy lies down on the floor and does breathing exercises every single day.

Kathy made a commitment to invite her kids to do an activity with her once a week. They were super into this because they loved their mom, but just hadn't understood how to handle her. They went line dancing one week and, in general, there was a sense of play that they had never collectively experienced before. Kathy even began to ask her kids for what she needed. She was using her voice and developing a sense of identity, which was huge.

As Kathy learned to nurture, she decided to get a King Charles puppy. She brought him into a session with her one day and it was so amazing to watch her nurture this animal.

It was really exciting when Kathy's nervous system calmed to the point where she was able to socially engage. Of course, this didn't come easily at first, because it was a new behavior, but Kathy was willing to put in the work. By the time she came to see me, Kathy did not have a lot of hope for her future. And Kathy did want to live—it's just that her current situation was no longer tolerable. Kathy joined a dog club with other King Charles dog owners, and it served as a way for her to socialize. She started spending time at the dog park and also getting out every day and walking. Suddenly, Kathy was mobilizing in healthy ways and mobilization was to combat her depression. While I encouraged Kathy, my sense was that she in some way intuitively knew that in order to feel more joy she was going to have to feel a sense of herself in movement.

Since Kathy wasn't working, she decided to take a course

at the local college. She also began taking yoga classes. She began to connect with different kinds of people in varied settings. As Kathy grew safer and safer in her own system, she realized that she had the capacity to feel joy, and understood that joy came through mobilization without fear and connection.

I could hardly contain myself when, about a year and a half after we started treatment, Kathy met someone. They hiked and did a lot of activities together. She took it very slowly because she was still scared. Sometimes she still sensed danger where it was not present. And, for understandable reasons, she still had a difficult time trusting. Because of all of this, Kathy would bring her boyfriend in close, then push him away. Then, after a while, she came to realize that she had her own life so, if this relationship worked out, that would be great. But, if not, it wasn't the end of the world. Luckily, this guy was madly in love with Kathy, and they were able to work through a lot of issues together. Today, Kathy and this new man are living together. They have a very nice relationship although, every once in a while, she freaks out and gets scared. It's almost as if her system doesn't trust that it's real. Here's the thing, though: Kathy now has the capacity and resilience to move through the discomfort and talk about it. She's aware that, for the first time, she's in a relationship where she's allowed to be herself. This is all very new, uncharted territory.

As for Kathy's digestive issues, they were resolved. We know that the digestive system can shut down when we are under threat. Once Kathy was able to feel a sense of safety, her digestive system was able to come back online.

Recently, Kathy decided to go back to work and is very happy at her job. It has allowed her to realize she's good at something. There, too, she sometimes gets scared but, again, she now knows how to work through it. She's not running away or shutting down. And even when she's scared, she's able to keep her social engagement system up and running, rather than being swept away into fight or flight.

## THE TAKEAWAY

It's important to be clear that depression can stem from different places. Some varieties of depression are chemical and require medication. Kathy did not happen to fall into that category; her depression was brought on through ongoing situational experiences and a stressed and exhausted nervous system.

Movement often helps with depression, but it has to be movement that is not borne of fear, and this requires working with the vagus nerve. The vagus nerve contributes to the regulation of our nervous system and is responsible for certain sensory and motor functions. It also helps with fear management.

Also imperative is that those who are struggling with depression find a safe face-to-face connection—that is one of the greatest healers. I am emphasizing face-to-face here, because while connecting with someone on the phone or digitally might help a little, it does not tend to help in the way that in-person connection does. So often, depression is tied up in a feeling of a lack of safety, which causes people to shut down and shut others out. I completely understand that when a person is in the throes of depression, this can be a big ask; however, I still advise people to white knuckle it and find a way to get out and connect with a safe person. You are never going to feel worse for having done so.

Also, each time you mobilize through depression, you actively build more resilience. You are teaching your body a new language—*to move through it.*

## HEALING FROM ANXIETY

Whereas depression makes it hard to mobilize, anxiety makes it difficult to taper down. I had a client named Anna who only had two gears: doing, doing, doing, and total exhaustion. Her anxiety was so bad that she had very little ability to be present with her kids without yelling at them because everything felt so out of control.

Anna grew up as one of nine kids. While things appeared

normal to the outside eye, there was actually a lot of emotional neglect in Anna's childhood home. No one ever validated Anna's experiences or cared about what she was feeling. Everything was black and white, with no acknowledgment for individual feelings or preferences. She always had to be doing something and, in the rare moments when she wasn't, Anna was scolded. It was definitively not a nurturing environment. So, Anna grew up with a lot of fear, and her way of dealing with life was to remain in constant motion; if she was doing, Anna didn't have to be feeling. She was completely overly mobilized. This was her version of fight or flight: constant flight. As a result, Anna's adrenaline, stress hormones, and cortisol were constantly pumping through her body. Doing was the only way she could feel safe or even moderately okay.

Anna came to me with the question a lot of people grappling with anxiety do: "What do I do? How are you going to fix it?"

## THE TREATMENT

For about six months straight, Anna blew into each of our sessions in a flurry, saying, "I'm so anxious, I'm so anxious, I'm so anxious."

"Okay," I replied slowly and calmly every time. "Tell me what you're doing when you're anxious."

Each time, Anna would present the latest series of details leading to her anxiety. Each time, she ended that explanation by asking me, "*Well*, what do I do with it?"

"Let's do an experiment," I told her. "Let's see what happens if we do nothing with it."

For an anxious person, this is an almost incomprehensible suggestion because of the energy pumping through them. Anxious people tend to have the inherent (although often subconscious) belief that if they don't mobilize, they're going to die. They are moving for survival. So, the trick is slowing down. Shifting out of mobilization and into observation sounds easy enough, but for those with anxiety it's a process of tapering. For example, Anna might come to a session telling me she has eight things on her to-do list. I will ask her to practice doing only four of them, and then observe what it feels like to stop once she completes that fourth item.

This wasn't easy for Anna. For a long time, she continued doing anything she could to avoid slowing down. Let's say she had a birthday party for one of her kids: Anna would become fixated on the decorations in an over-the-top kind of way that kept her going, going, going. There was always something to keep Anna running around until she finally reached the point where she collapsed from total exhaustion.

Anxious people also tend to live in the past or ruminate about the future. Both of these are a way of staying out of the present moment, which is a place where people with anxiety have a very difficult time residing. Being in either the future or the past allows those in the throes of anxiety to stay out of the present moment, which would necessitate them to come into their body. That is why I encouraged Anna to *observe*. I wanted her to practice being here and now, even if here and now felt uncomfortable.

Anna and I spent a lot of time discussing how she felt, knowing that she wasn't doing all of the things she felt compelled to do. "My stomach is rumbling," she would tell me, or "I feel tightness in my chest." From there it was a matter of staying with that feeling. I would ask Anna to put her hand on her chest and accept and hold space for that anxiety. Not only does observation help to connect a person with their body, but it also tends to slow things down.

Anna began to realize that she could feel anxious and move through that anxiety without having to act upon it. It was from this point that she started to gain the ability to mobilize without fear. She was able to act more slowly and methodically, without a constant feeling of frenzy. She even came to the realization that no one—including herself—was going to die if she didn't get something done. This allowed Anna to become more fluid, embodied, and tolerant. With all of this, the anxiety didn't completely diminish, but it did begin to lose its charge.

With lower levels of anxiety, Anna had more tolerance for the inherent unpredictabilities of life. This allowed her to be more present with her children, as well as less agitated by them. She got to the point where she could even be playful with them. She also started to establish a stronger connection with her husband, and they can now more easily work through issues when they arise because Anna is able to articulate her experience in a way that she couldn't do before. The same can be said for all of her relationships, actually. Today, Anna has real and far more meaningful connections with her friends than she ever did before, because she is able to set better boundaries by vocalizing what does and doesn't work for her as opposed to simply going into fight or flight mode. She is able to remain socially engaged, even when her nervous system is activated.

Perhaps most important of all (and at the root of all of this), is the fact that Anna has begun to develop a relationship with herself. She can be with herself and observe what is happening in her body and in her nervous system, and then put that experience into words.

THE TAKEAWAY

As with Anna, it's important for anyone dealing with anxiety to build up the tolerance necessary to slow things down and become their own observer. Breathwork helps with this a lot, because it calms the nervous system and brings us back into our body. It draws us directly into the present moment. This is huge when it comes to alleviating anxiety, which tends to cause us to hover above our bodies, almost as if we're not really there. We disconnect.

As with any other variety of healing, overcoming anxiety requires that we have the desire and motivation to want to heal. If you are reading this book, I am guessing that you do have this desire. You likely feel uncomfortable with where you are and feel that something needs to shift. Acknowledging that you are tired of feeling the way you are feeling right now is the first step in all of this.

## HEALING FROM CHRONIC PAIN

Jeffrey was in bad shape when he first found me. He had recently completed treatment for cancer, and it left him feeling severely depressed and suicidal. With this, Jeffrey had become very fearful and was experiencing chronic pain.

Once I began working with Jeffrey, it became apparent that no one had made clear to him what the aftereffects of chemo and radiation would be. He was caught off guard by the chronic pain in his joints and neuropathy in his hands and feet that the treatment had left in its wake. And these were just the physical side-effects. There were emotional ones, too.

Before the treatment began, Jeffrey struggled to get a diagnosis. It took Jeffrey two years between the time he first went to see the doctor about several odd symptoms and the actual cancer diagnosis. For twenty-four months, the doctors continued to tell Jeffrey that he was okay. Even though he intuitively knew something wasn't right, Jeffrey went along with it for all that time and didn't press them to dig deeper, nor did he get a second opinion. Jeffrey felt a lot of shame around the fact that he had "allowed" himself to get into this situation. In addition to that, the pain Jeffrey experienced following treatment scared him and left him with images of the cancer spreading further. Jeffrey had been in a relationship that ended right before he found out he was sick. Not only that, but Jeffrey's cousin—who had always been his "safe place"—didn't show up to support him. Instead, Jeffrey found himself feeling alone and disappointed throughout the course of this very scary experience.

Before the cancer, Jeffrey's life had seemed okay, but now he was left feeling unsafe and alone. At least that's how Jeffrey perceived his situation to be. But the more we worked together, the more apparent it became that Jeffrey had never felt a significant attachment to himself and, likely as a result, had been in and out of several relationships. At the root of this was the fact that Jeffrey had never really learned to articulate his needs.

I see this a lot in my patients who have undergone developmental trauma or stress during early childhood: they begin to disconnect from themselves and never fully develop a sense of autonomy. Likewise, Jeffrey never developed a great sense of boundaries or even an understanding of what he needed to feel safe in life. This manifested in his recent cancer scare: Jeffrey didn't know what he needed, so he didn't ask questions of the doctors or argue with those things he didn't agree with. Jeffrey had never learned to take charge of or responsibility for himself. He didn't know how to use his voice. This same dynamic had manifested in all areas of Jeffrey's life. Even when relationships weren't working for him, Jeffrey stayed in them because he did not know how to speak up for himself and his needs.

Jeffrey had been an athlete for his entire life, but after treatment he found that he was unable to sense his own body. It was almost like he had lost the ability to be in his body. He could no longer withstand any amount of physical activity without experiencing a massive amount of anxiety and an increase in digestive issues he had for many years. It got to the point where Jeffrey couldn't really function in a meaningful way.

Despite the fact that Jeffrey was fifty years old when I met him, I had to teach him the basics of relationships and boundaries. Before we began bodywork, it was imperative that Jeffrey and I establish a sense of trust and safety. To do this, I did a lot of education about boundaries, healthy relationships, and the importance of Jeffrey being his own advocate and taking charge of his medical decisions moving forward. I made it clear that I would be a sounding board in this process. As we discussed these issues, I would ask Jeffrey what he noticed in his body and where he could feel emotion or sensation cropping up. Jeffrey couldn't feel a thing. The only thing he could feel was the pain the cancer had left behind. And every time he felt the pain, his mind went directly to the worst-case scenario and his digestive issues got worse.

Once Jeffrey and I discussed the reasons why fear is nothing more than a projection of a story, it was time to shift that understanding into his body through a felt sense of safety. This process began with me letting Jeffrey know that I heard him. I heard and understood where he was coming from and why he felt the way that he did.

I came to understand that Jeffrey's inability to feel his body was a result of fear. Fear that any feeling meant that he was sick again or that he was going to get worse.

Anything that he *did* manage to feel in his body resulted in a sense of complete overwhelm and a surge of anxiety.

Through touchwork, I was able to help Jeffrey move back into his body. I began by helping him build up a sense of safety. We used different interventions, including breathwork. I physically held the place on his body that hurt while he breathed into that space. We got to the point where Jeffrey was able to help regulate his nervous system by engaging in diaphragmatic breath, which is very effective in managing and decreasing stress and anxiety.

We also discovered that the sensation of heat made Jeffrey feel safe, so we began to work with that. I placed heating pads on Jeffrey's stomach, neck, or wherever he was feeling pain. The heat allowed him to experience the pain in what he interpreted as a safe way and, also, put him in a position to specifically identify and put a voice to where his pain was.

Interestingly, Jeffrey was a successful businessman and had no problem trusting his gut or speaking up in that realm of his life. I used business scenarios to get Jeffrey to drop into his body and notice what it felt like when something was "right" or "wrong." Over time, he learned to translate those same feelings and subsequent actions and reactions to his personal life.

I also guided Jeffrey through the process of taking charge of his own health and wellness. Jeffrey began seeing a naturopath I referred him to and, after a while, when physical issues came up, I suggested that Jeffrey take that issue to the naturopath. I also recommended that Jeffrey contribute his own opinions about what he did and did not want to do when consulting with the doctor.

When Jeffrey's pain kicked up, I had him call his friend, Jack, who felt safe. During these times, Jack came over to Jeffrey's house with his dog, and Jeffrey touched the dog with his hands and feet. This was particularly effective because of Jeffrey's neuropathy. It gave him a sense of being able to use his hands and feet in a tactile way that felt comfortable.

These multiple practices gave Jeffrey a new way to begin building a safe container within himself and to establish a sense of responsibility for his own care. He learned to trust his own experience to gain an understanding of what felt right and wrong for him.

Today, Jeffrey's pain is not gone, but it is better. The neuropathy is not nearly as bad as it was. When I first met Jeffrey, his pain levels were somewhere between an eight or ten on a daily basis. Today, they hover around a four and never progress beyond a six. With this alleviation of pain, Jeffrey has learned to connect to his body from a place of joy rather than fear.

After we built up Jeffrey's autonomy, we began to look at his fear of being alone. There, we found something ironic: while Jeffrey had a deep fear of being alone, he also had no tolerance for the way in which many of the people in his life behaved with him. These were people who Jeffrey had been friends with for years. We continued to work with boundaries, and Jeffrey set about establishing them with people in his life who were pushing him around or taking advantage of him. It was incredible to see Jeffrey realize through the process of doing this that he didn't have to tolerate people's bullshit. He could surround himself with people whom he wanted to be around. Jeffrey did all of this in a polite way, but also stopped caring so much about whether or not he offended someone in the process of establishing boundaries.

And then an even more amazing thing happened: Jeffrey realized that he actually loved having his own space. He loved living alone and making decisions for himself. He found that he had more energy to put himself out there and develop new, incredible, healthy, and supportive friendships. I believe Jeffrey was able to accomplish this because he was able to individualize. He became autonomous and learned to enjoy his life, his freedom, and his space, which left him with plenty of room to emotionally connect to the people he wanted to connect with. In other words, to form healthy attachments.

Jeffrey shows us that even when pain is present, what matters most is how our nervous system manages that pain. When a person cannot find a sense of safety amidst pain, their nervous system further activates, resulting in greater intensity. The calmer the nervous system is, the greater the capacity to manage the intensity of pain. This goes back to the idea of interoception: the more heightened the experience of pain is, the less accurately we can assess it.

Because of the body's innate ability to turn on its survival mechanisms, it is easy for us to go into fight, flight, or freeze when we experience intense pain. This only produces more stress hormones and only serves to produce more inflammation in the body. Inflammation causes pain. I'm sure you can see the vicious cycle this creates.

Also, never discount the importance of connection when it comes to healing. Remember, pain is not just physical, it is emotional. And healthy connections and attachments positively impact our wellness.

## HEALING FROM DISORDERED EATING

When I first met Candy, she was so dissociated that she was unable to be in the room with me in any way other than the most literal physical sense. It was almost impossible for her to track what I was saying, let alone what she was saying. Candy had no awareness of space and time, and had reached a place of such distrust and disconnection that it took nearly six months before she was even able to orient herself in the room.

For our work to be effective, I needed Candy to feel as safe as possible, so I had to allow her to dissociate during our interactions, then slowly and gently bring her in for short amounts of time. Drawing Candy in involved the simplest of things, like having her notice a color in the room. It took months to move beyond this.

Of course, Candy didn't get to this point of dissociation by accident. She had a severe history of trauma that involved sexual abuse from a very young age when her mother remarried. Candy's mother was manipulative and ignored what was going on right in front of her. The sexual abuse and rape continued from various people through the time Candy was in her early twenties. She had fallen into disordered eating patterns from as young as eight—not coincidentally, the same age she was when the abuse started.

Despite all of this, Candy went to college and had a good job working from home, which felt safe for her. As a thirty-something-year-old woman, Candy was caring for and housing the five foster children her mother had adopted over the years, as well as her mother, who was no longer able to care for herself or the kids she had taken on, due to illness.

I know this story because it dribbled out over time as Candy grew to trust me more and more. I never pushed it, just as I never push the story with any of my clients because, as a Somatic Experiencing practitioner, knowing the details about someone's history is only important in the sense of serving as an empathic witness. I don't need the full story for the healing to occur. Plus, the process of obtaining these details can be incredibly triggering for a patient and push them right back down into the trauma vortex. But when they *do* want to share because it feels good to be heard by a trusted person, I am happy to hold that space for them. Everyone needs an empathic witness to heal.

Through all of this, Candy's struggle with bulimia continued. For her, it was a way of feeling a sense of comfort and regulating her nervous system. She would stuff herself, then purge for the sensation of feeling empty and light—to her, this was freedom. It allowed Candy an avenue through which to dissociate from her real-life situation and was also a way of punishing her body, which had caused her so much pain. By the time I met her, bulimia had been Candy's constant for more than two decades.

## THE TREATMENT

It was obvious that Candy needed and would benefit from touch and somatic work, but I also quickly realized that she was not yet at a place where she could tolerate it. Touch would only make her feel less safe. For a person with Candy's history, you can probably imagine how threatening it must feel to have your body touched or to be pushed into it in an unwanted way.

This meant Candy and I had to take another tactic to get her into her body. For us, this involved developing awareness to counteract the dissociation. We were able to bring awareness to the fact that Candy was dissociated from her body in the first place. "What does it feel like to lose track of time and space?" I might ask her. We took this route because, from an early age, Candy had learned that emotions were dangerous. She didn't want to identify, much less feel them. Beginning with questions like this, over time, Candy was able to connect to herself and put words to her experience in ways that were extremely articulate. We both learned that, when Candy allowed herself to lean into her emotional experiences, she knew exactly how she was feeling and could express that very specifically.

As we worked together, I came to realize that Candy was always either playing with her hair or touching something. It was obvious that she used her tactile sense to self-regulate. I felt this was a great entry point to help her connect with her physical sense of self in a way that didn't feel threatening. I did this by bringing various objects in for her to touch and then describe. I noticed that every time we performed this exercise, Candy's anxiety decreased. The practice of touching and describing brought Candy into the present moment and allowed her to connect with her own sensory experience.

Through this process, we got to the point where Candy was able to stay in the room with me. Over time, she began talking more and more about her experiences. With this, her favorite expression was, "I don't know."

"You *do* know," I would gently encourage her. "So, let's slow down and notice what's happening in your body now as you talk."

"I feel anxious," she might reply. And then Candy would explain specifically how and where she felt that anxiety in her body.

Candy and I made progress, but over time it became clear to me that her living situation was too triggering. I convinced Candy that she should go to an inpatient facility where she could live separately from her mother and the children. The biggest part of this is that we had established enough trust that Candy was able to allow me to direct her treatment. Candy agreed to go to an inpatient program where she could get the appropriate level of care. Over the course of the next six months, Candy lived in the inpatient center. During that time, I stayed in touch with Candy and made sure she knew that I would be there when she returned. I'm so happy to say that Candy has been out of the treatment facility for a year and is behavior free, with the exception of one slip-up over the holidays. And even that represented a massive turning point for Candy because she got right back on track with the understanding that she has the ability to take responsibility for what she wants and how she wants to treat her body.

Candy and I have even gotten to the point where we can do touch sessions. This started by small measures, with the two of us simply sitting shoulder-to-shoulder for a few minutes. After our first session doing this Candy messaged me, and wrote, "This was by far the best session I've ever had. I would have flipped my lid had we done this six months ago. Although quite uncomfortable, I don't feel like I have to engage in any behaviors. I don't have to isolate. I didn't have a panic attack. Before, I would have scrubbed and boiled my skin raw in a hot shower. But I'm okay. I'm stable and I don't feel crazy. Isn't that amazing?"

Candy and I continue to take seemingly small steps

forward that represent massive breakthroughs for her. During some sessions I touch her brainstem, where her reptilian brain lives; other times, we might sit with our feet together. It is incredible to witness her body language begin to shift as Candy becomes more relaxed in and at one with her body.

## WHAT IT ALL MEANS

Until fairly recently, the majority of eating disorder treatments were focused on cognitive and behavioral changes, as well as body image issues. In my opinion, eating disorder treatments need to go beyond these components for healing to be complete.

Trauma is often the culprit of eating disorders. I have never met a person with an eating disorder who does not have a history of chronic stress. What we really need to focus on is resolving the trauma locked in the body. In doing so we can assist individuals in building safety in the body, so they do not need to use maladaptive behaviors to regulate their systems. When we talk about body image, we are tackling the brain; what we need to address here is the body and the discomfort a person is feeling inside of themselves.

This is not my theory alone, but an important emerging point of research regarding interoception. When we get to the heart of the interoceptive experience, we can shift things for a patient in order to create a more accurate perspective and experience. We are also seeing a significant connection between the interoceptive experience and emotional regulation.

Common with eating disordered patients is a lack of trust or connection with the world. As a result, their primary relationship becomes the relationship they have with food, whether that involves starving themselves, binging, purging, or any combination of these three. We need to find a way to make these patients feel safe and, again, that is an embodied experience. When a person begins to see the world as even a little bit of a safer place, they have more capacity to connect. Once they can do this, disordered eating patterns become less dominant. The voice of the eating disorder becomes more muted as the voice of one's authentic voice comes through. Additionally, the patient is then able to create healthy relationships and attachments with others and move forward in their life.

## HEALING RIGIDITY

Rigidity is the behavior people exhibit when they are so constricted in their day-to-day life that they cannot lift themselves above their routine and organization. It can be paralyzing and, even on a more mundane level, completely suck the joy out of life.

Sarah, who was extremely rigid, came to me as a super successful entrepreneur in her early thirties. Sarah was the product of a very chaotic home that included an alcoholic, womanizing father and a depressed mother, who ultimately received a cancer diagnosis and emerged from treatment even more depressed than she had been to start. Sarah's early experiences taught her that she didn't want to ever be in a position where she had to rely on anyone. From an early age, Sarah became super independent and was very clear on the fact that this was the only way she could survive life.

Speaking of survival, Sarah's nervous system was in a perpetual state of survival and adrenaline pump. In some ways, this paid off. By her early twenties, Sarah was making seven hundred thousand dollars per year. By all appearances, Sarah had everything—she was wealthy, super smart, and gorgeous. What people couldn't see is that Sarah thrived in the chaos of her professional life because her nervous system was in constant overdrive. Chaos was the only environment she knew how to function in.

When I met Sarah, she had just given birth to a special needs baby who had various issues. As a result, everything felt irritating to Sarah. She had no patience for anyone or anything else besides her child. It was clear that her general vibe was, "Don't fuck with me, and get the fuck out of my way while you're at it." Sarah's schedule had always been her bible, and it was even more so now that she had this additional responsibility to juggle.

In addition to all of this, Sarah felt like a victim. Her boyfriend, who was the father of her child, wasn't necessarily the best partner. Sarah stayed with him but fixated on everything that was wrong in the relationship. It was almost as if the chaos somehow regulated her nervous system. After all, that's the type of environment in which she was brought up.

## THE TREATMENT

The work in front of Sarah and I was to get her nervous system to regulate in the absence of chaos. This involved teaching Sarah's nervous system how to function comfortably without chaos. She had to learn how to tolerate life when things weren't in order. She was using rigid behaviors as a way of containing all of the things around her that felt unmanageable and beyond her control. Her nervous system needed to be recalibrated to learn how to function in a healthy window of tolerance. For Sarah, this meant bringing her nervous system down by about ten notches.

Part of the way Sarah coped up to this point was by disconnecting from her body (is this beginning to sound familiar?). It was like she existed in a constant state of hovering ten feet above her physical being. Sarah was in such a removed state that she couldn't even decipher when she was hungry or full.

When Sarah felt particularly dysregulated, she shifted into an even greater mode of overdrive, doing, doing, doing, doing. I knew that the one place Sarah could ground herself and feel safe was when she was with her baby. Together we worked on getting Sarah to recognize when she felt overwhelmed and, when she did, to go spend time outside in nature with her baby, where she could slow down and be present as opposed to ramping up and hovering higher and higher above herself.

To others, our sessions might have looked like Sarah and I were just two women and a baby out for a stroll, because that's what we spent a lot of our time together doing. Sometimes during these walks, I would check in, but always while we were still in motion. When we stopped, Sarah simply became too activated. "Tell me what you're noticing around you right now," I would say.

Once Sarah became more accustomed to this practice, we started the big work, which was getting Sarah to focus on herself and her journey. She had to become safe enough within herself to understand that she couldn't control everything outside of her. Sarah couldn't control her boyfriend, she couldn't control her mom; she could only control herself.

Sarah also had to learn to trust her own sensory experiences rather than allowing them to overwhelm her entire system. Sarah didn't trust a lot of people, which threw her into a state of great discomfort and activation. When this happened, I had Sarah call me so that we could work on orienting and grounding her. This was as simple as having Sarah feel her feet on the ground or listen to music or the sounds around her. She had to learn to drop into her own senses, but in a way that calmed and soothed her, rather than making her want to run. Even in small increments, this began to build more resilience within Sarah so that she could come into her body, move through discomfort, and be with the experience at hand without attempting to control it or run off into ten different directions all at the same time.

This work shouldn't feel hard, because as we continue to practice these new behaviors on a consistent basis, our nervous system begins to learn something new. It starts to learn what it feels like to settle, and settling is soothing. It is your nervous system's natural state, so it *wants* to go there, and can teach itself to go there naturally when it is provided some space and a little bit of instruction along the way.

At first, Sarah was confused by the sense of calm she felt after our sessions. From there, we began to build up to the practice of getting Sarah into that space of calm in the moment of activation. Sarah might call me all wound up and I would have her do an experiment. "Tell me that story again, but see if you can slow it down while you tell it," I would tell her. Sarah soon discovered that doing something as simple as speaking more slowly could have a positive net impact in terms of regulating her nervous system. In fact, this is how I speak to my clients—slowly and softly. It's not by accident, because I know that just as our own even voices can regulate the nervous system, so, too, can the voice of another person. On some level, we all know this: think about how you feel when you have a conversation with someone who is all amped up versus when someone conveys information in a slower, softer way.

I then began teaching Sarah to let go of her need for solutions. What would it feel like if she *didn't* feel a sense of ownership to fix every single problem she saw around her? For Sarah, the answer was that it felt uncomfortable. So, we experimented with sitting in that discomfort and allowing others to solve their own issues rather than Sarah jumping in and taking the reins.

The more Sarah practiced focusing on herself and her baby, the more she was able to stay out of a reactive state.

The more she was able to refrain from attempting to take control of everything and everyone around her. And the more she was able to set boundaries without going into a rage.

As all of this happened, Sarah stopped trying to control her boyfriend and realized he would do whatever he was going to do. She also understood that she could make her decisions from there. Ultimately, Sarah chose to end that relationship and today her life is thriving.

Today when Sarah comes in, we don't have to walk or remain in constant motion anymore. We can simply sit down and chat calmly for a half hour, then Sarah jumps on the table while I do some somatic work to relax her. I tend to focus a lot on Sarah's brainstem, where her overactive fight or flight responses reside. I'm happy to tell you that, today, Sarah is not nearly as reactive as she used to be. She is able to let go and ride the waves in ways that would have been inconceivable earlier in her life.

## WHAT IT ALL MEANS

Here's the thing about rigidity: it *feels* safe. It feels like a mechanism to keep the world under control. The problem is that it offers a false sense of safety and it can completely rob a person of the ability to ever experience a sense of embodiment, fluidity, or true joy. Rigidity is also very literal; people who execute these behaviors generally have a body that is full of constriction. It's difficult to move within that, and it certainly doesn't feel good. Rigidity opens the door to a lot of dysregulation in the nervous system, because rigid people become dysregulated when things don't go their way. And, in the real world, things often don't go our way.

If you experience rigidity in your own life, stop and think for a second about how nice it would feel to be able to move *with* your circumstances rather than constantly pressing back against them. Even when things aren't perfect. How much more ease and fluidity might you feel on a moment-by-moment basis? How much gentler would the world and your own body seem? And, really, how much more productive could you actually be without constantly fighting an uphill battle against stress?

To get to this point, we must learn to tolerate and build resilience around the discomfort that is required to learn to let things go. To let other people and circumstances and the world be as they are going to be without our intervention. We must learn to stop constantly pushing. At first, this will feel like a complete loss of control and safety, but the truth is that rigid behaviors create neither control nor safety. In fact, they often create the opposite. That sense of control and safety were never real to begin with.

## YOU'VE ALREADY TAKEN THE FIRST STEP

The one thing each of the clients in these stories of healing have in common is that they were willing to do the work. For all of them this meant, quite literally, facing up to their biggest fears. It required them to come to a point where they realized that confronting their pain head on in the short term was the best way to alleviate further pain in the future (or, at least, to have the tools to work through pain more quickly in the future). It meant getting un-stuck. It's also important to note that many of these clients embarked upon a process of becoming unstuck from situations they had been existing in for a very long time.

Getting unstuck and moving forward all begins with one step. That first step leads to the next step and so on and so forth until, at last, you realize that you are changed. You are free. You are alive in ways you never could have dreamed of before.

You will notice that none of these clients found a quick fix; that's because quick fixes don't work. However, they *did* find a way to overhaul their lives through a series of changes that actually feel quite organic and fluid once you decide that you are ready to make them.

PART TWO

CREATING
CHANGE

# CHAPTER FIVE

# ASSESSING YOUR PROBLEM BEHAVIORS

Now that we've seen what trauma and its impact look like in the nervous system as well as how to heal, let's begin to apply this information to your own life and healing.

In this chapter you will find a series of assessments that identify the five most common manifestations of distress in the nervous system. These assessments are designed to help you begin to put together the puzzle of your own nervous system. Through doing this, you can begin to gain a clearer understanding of how your nervous system is currently functioning and, from there, understand what you need to do in order to create more systemic regulation.

This is important to know because the specific way in which your nervous system is dysregulated dictates the interventions for healing. For example, if you tend to go into a fight or flight state, you need a treatment that will allow you to slow things down. If, on the other hand, you tend to freeze, you require a treatment that will help you mobilize without fear.

Approaching wellness from this perspective is different from receiving a diagnosis in talk therapy because it does not involve how-tos. Instead, this information is designed to spark curiosity about yourself, your life, and how you relate to the world and to other people. It's designed to help you understand how your nervous system is functioning and to make you aware of what's happening when your responses kick in. It's about helping you become more attuned to yourself on a sensory level. Once you do this, you will gain a greater capacity to see how these pieces might be getting in the way of living a more embodied life, and a life with more vitality.

How-tos are really just shortcuts. They don't allow us to get to the root of the problem or to gain a real understanding of how our nervous system is functioning. They are a Band-Aid, not a fix.

## HOW ASSESSMENTS WORK

In the following pages, you will find a series of questions for you to answer. Do not get overly analytical in doing so. Answer with the first thing that comes to mind. Your first answer will almost always be the most accurate.

The assessments that follow are all linked to how the nervous system functions. They are research-based and aligned with peer-reviewed, published work. In other words, they are based on real science.

As you consider the statements in each assessment, consider your typical experience over the course of the past twelve months and choose the response that best fits. If the statement does not relate to your life in the past twelve months, you may think back to the last time you had a similar experience.

It is neither better nor worse if you have a high or low score; what is important is that you are taking care of yourself and learning more about your mental and emotional health. If at any point in taking this survey you begin to feel uncomfortable, please take a break and come back when you are feeling better.

These assessments are also available online at movingbeyondtrauma.co.

## ASSESSMENT #1: FIGHT, FLIGHT, OR FREEZE

In this day and age, almost everyone has experienced a situation that feels either threatening, traumatic, or stressful. The body has a built-in process to help us handle these moments through the nervous system. When our body senses a potential threat, our nervous system engages one or more of several responses. First, the body tends toward flight or fight. First, our body propels us to attempt to flee and run to safety. When fleeing is not an option, fight kicks in as the next defense. This includes arguing, yelling and screaming, physically attacking, and fighting. When neither flight nor fight are possible, freeze is the next best option. We become paralyzed, motionless, or speechless. Previous experiences, gender, and age can also help shape how the body responds.

Each response includes different physical symptoms and engages specific elements of the nervous system, areas of the brain, and hormones. Many individuals have a dominant response, though some tend toward two, or even all three. None of these responses is better or worse than any other; all of them are important and necessary for our survival. However, when unprocessed past trauma is present, the system can become stuck in fight, flight, or freeze. These responses can become or remain activated in everyday situations or experiences that trigger reminders of previous traumas.

This scale is meant to help you understand your personal tendencies.

## FIGHT

1. I have been told that I tend to use a defensive tone in the course of regular conversation.
   a. Always
   b. Often
   c. Sometimes
   d. Rarely
   e. Never

2. When someone hurts me, I retaliate.
   a. Always
   b. Often
   c. Sometimes
   d. Rarely
   e. Never

3. I fight back when I experience a real or perceived threat.
   a. Always
   b. Often
   c. Sometimes
   d. Rarely
   e. Never

4. When I am criticized, I react defensively.
   a. Always
   b. Often
   c. Sometimes

d. Rarely

e. Never

5. I think retaliation is often the best form of defense.

    a. Always

    b. Often

    c. Sometimes

    d. Rarely

    e. Never

6. People are always provoking me.

    a. Always

    b. Often

    c. Sometimes

    d. Rarely

    e. Never

7. I tend to overreact to situations.

    a. Always

    b. Often

    c. Sometimes

    d. Rarely

    e. Never

8. I tend to have angry outbursts.

    a. Always

    b. Often

    c. Sometimes

    d. Rarely

    e. Never

9. When I argue with others, it tends to be long and drawn out, sometimes lasting several hours or days.

a. Always

b. Often

c. Sometimes

d. Rarely

e. Never

10. Others are afraid to approach me, unsure of how I might react.

a. Always

b. Often

c. Sometimes

d. Rarely

e. Never

## FLIGHT

1. When I sense danger, I try to get away as fast as possible.

a. Always

b. Often

c. Sometimes

d. Rarely

e. Never

2. When I see an unfriendly-looking stranger, I try to avoid them.

a. Always

b. Often

c. Sometimes

d. Rarely

e. Never

3. I tend to storm out of the house during an argument.

a. Always

b. Often

c. Sometimes

d. Rarely

e. Never

4. When I start feeling uncomfortable, I try to leave the situation as quickly as possible.

a. Always

b. Often

c. Sometimes

d. Rarely

e. Never

5. I try my best to avoid confrontation.

a. Always

b. Often

c. Sometimes

d. Rarely

e. Never

6. When a fire alarm goes off, I quickly evacuate.

a. Always

b. Often

c. Sometimes

d. Rarely

e. Never

7. I quickly move away when I feel that others are invading my personal space.

a. Always

b. Often

c. Sometimes

d. Rarely

e. Never

8. When people are fighting in my presence, I try to remove myself from the situation as quickly as possible.

   a. Always

   b. Often

   c. Sometimes

   d. Rarely

   e. Never

9. I rush away at the first sign of danger.

   a. Always

   b. Often

   c. Sometimes

   d. Rarely

   e. Never

10. I leave as soon as possible when I feel socially awkward.

    a. Always

    b. Often

    c. Sometimes

    d. Rarely

    e. Never

### FREEZE

1. When I sense danger, I feel physically paralyzed or stuck.

   a. Always

   b. Often

   c. Sometimes

d. Rarely

e. Never

2. My mind feels blocked when I am being criticized.

    a. Always

    b. Often

    c. Sometimes

    d. Rarely

    e. Never

3. I lose my words around certain people.

    a. Always

    b. Often

    c. Sometimes

    d. Rarely

    e. Never

4. Even when I know what I want to say, sometimes the words won't come out.

    a. Always

    b. Often

    c. Sometimes

    d. Rarely

    e. Never

5. I stay very still in my bed when I hear strange sounds at night.

    a. Always

    b. Often

    c. Sometimes

    d. Rarely

    e. Never

6. My body gets stiff when I feel scared.

    a. Always

    b. Often

    c. Sometimes

    d. Rarely

    e. Never

7. The mere presence of certain people or things paralyzes me.

    a. Always

    b. Often

    c. Sometimes

    d. Rarely

    e. Never

8. I don't know how to respond when a stranger unexpectedly speaks to me.

    a. Always

    b. Often

    c. Sometimes

    d. Rarely

    e. Never

9. I feel frozen with fear when someone confronts me.

    a. Always

    b. Often

    c. Sometimes

    d. Rarely

    e. Never

10. When I am scared, it's as if my brain stops working.

    a. Always

b. Often

c. Sometimes

d. Rarely

e. Never

## Scoring[2]

Count the number of responses you have for each letter and record that number next to the corresponding letter. Multiply the number of each response by its designated number of points. Finally, add up each subtotal to calculate your final scores.

Note the range in which your score lands. We will use these scores as the basis for incorporating a healing-exercise program in the following chapter.

| Fight | Flight | Freeze |
|---|---|---|
| A ____ x 5 = ____ | A ____ x 5 = ____ | A ____ x 5 = ____ |
| B ____ x 4 = ____ | B ____ x 4 = ____ | B ____ x 4 = ____ |

---

2    A number of existing measures for the fight-flight-freeze response were consulted in the creation of this scale. This scale borrows Fight Q5 (Corr and Cooper, 2016), Freeze Q1 (Reuter et al., 2015), and Freeze Q7 (Smederevac et al., 2014). Several existing measures were also edited to derive the final versions here: Fight Q2 (Jackson, 2009); Fight Q4, 8, and 9 (Jackson, 2009, Appendix A Item Pool), Fight Q5 (Reuter et al., 2015), Fight Q10 (Corr and Cooper, 2016), Freeze Q2 (Smederevac et al., 2014), Freeze Q5 (Jackson, 2009) and Freeze Q10 (Jackson, 2009, Appendix A Item Pool). All remaining items were created specifically for this scale.

C _____ x 3 = _____     C _____ x 3 = _____     C _____ x 3 = _____

D _____ x 2 = _____     D _____ x 2 = _____     D _____ x 2 = _____

E _____ x 1 = _____     E _____ x 1 = _____     E _____ x 1 = _____

TOTAL = _____          TOTAL = _____          TOTAL = _____

## 42-50 = Very High

A very high score means that this particular response is very common for you. This is neither good nor bad, it is simply the way your specific nervous system tends to respond when it senses you are under threat.

Many individuals have a dominant response, the one they tend toward most, though others may score on the higher end for more than one response, especially if they have a history of developmental trauma. You may find yourself easily triggered and going into fight, tending to argue or throw something when you're upset. If flight is very high, you may feel the urge to leave an uncomfortable situation ASAP or storm out during a confrontation. If freeze is very high, you may find yourself feeling, well, frozen and unable to act, think, or feel much of anything.

## 34-41 = High

A high score means this nervous system response occurs frequently. Perhaps you are already aware that you tend to get a bit aggressive, typically want to leave the scene of the crime when uncomfortable, or often find yourself feeling paralyzed. Or, this may be your first drop of awareness as to your particular patterns.

There is no right or wrong here. Remember your nervous system is always trying to protect and keep you safe, even if your response may seem out of proportion to the situation at hand. Whatever your response is, it likely feels like an automatic reaction right now, with little choice in how you respond to what is happening around you. In time and with practice, you will cultivate a greater sense of space and eventually may find yourself reacting less intensely.

### 26-33 = Medium

A medium score means your system likes this response, and that's perfectly okay. Everybody is different, and therefore each individual will have their own "profile" of nervous system reactions. This one just happens to be part of yours.

A medium score means you may only go into this response sometimes, while handling other situations more calmly. Or it may mean you go into this response often, but only at a mid-level strength. For instance, with fight you may feel the urge to kick or hit someone, but also remain aware enough to understand that it's not a good idea to actually do it. You may freeze only sometimes, or "thaw out" and return to a baseline easier than others.

What matters most is that you're here taking care of yourself. As you gain awareness, you'll also gain confidence and a wider range of choices when confronted with stressful or threatening scenarios in the future.

### 10-25 = Low

A low score indicates this response is not very relevant for you, though you may go into it at times. We all face challenges in life that feel like more than we can handle in the moment, so it may be that your nervous system tends toward fight, flight, or freeze only occasionally and under extenuating circumstances.

If you have higher scores on other responses, you will likely feel better faster by working on those first. If all of your scores are in the low range, that is a great sign you already have a lot of resilience built into your system.

## ASSESSMENT #2: TASK APPROACH

From time to time, we all have tasks on our plate that we just don't want to do, and which might even stir up some fear or anxiety. Despite this, a healthy individual approaches the task head-on and finds a way to work through it, despite their negative feelings. When unresolved trauma is present, however, the nervous system becomes over-involved and, as a way of protecting oneself from these uncomfortable feelings, a person might find themselves procrastinating.

Task-related fear and uncertainty can trigger two main responses: mobilization (fight-or-flight) or disengagement (shutdown). When an individual's fight-or-flight system is activated, mobilization can take on one of two forms: mobilizing in and mobilizing out. Mobilizing in means fight-or-flight energy is used to over-engage in a task. This can appear as obsessively checking every detail. Mobilizing out means fight-or-flight energy is instead used in an active avoidance of the task, causing a person to engage in busy-work activities, such as cleaning or organizing the night before a big exam as an excuse to avoid studying.

Another possible response is disengagement. When this occurs, a person's dorsal vagal nerve is activated, leading to shutdown and a sense of collapse. Individuals who experience this might find themselves zoning out, taking a nap, or binge-watching Netflix when they have an important task to do.

No matter how someone approaches anxiety-ridden tasks, compassion is important. While all of these forms of procrastination do have a negative impact, the behaviors are typically a subconscious attempt to protect oneself from overwhelming feelings. People will usually score higher on one response than the other, although in the case of complex trauma, any combination is possible.

## MOBILIZATION

1. When I have a task to complete, I become over-focused and obsessed until it is finished.
   a. Always
   b. Often
   c. Sometimes
   d. Rarely
   e. Never

2. When I am overwhelmed by a project, I respond by making sure I have everything correct.
   a. Always
   b. Often
   c. Sometimes
   d. Rarely
   e. Never

3. Nothing else in the world, including social engagements, exists when I have an important task to complete.
   a. Always
   b. Often
   c. Sometimes
   d. Rarely
   e. Never

4. I don't consider my work successful unless I've put in 150 percent effort.

a. Always

b. Often

c. Sometimes

d. Rarely

e. Never

5. My goal is to finish a project as soon as possible, regardless of when it is due.

a. Always

b. Often

c. Sometimes

d. Rarely

e. Never

6. I find myself active and busy with other things that keep me distracted from the task at hand.

a. Always

b. Often

c. Sometimes

d. Rarely

e. Never

7. When I have an overwhelming task, my go-to response is to exercise.

a. Always

b. Often

c. Sometimes

d. Rarely

e. Never

8. When someone is upset with me, I feel better after cleaning and organizing.

a. Always

b. Often

c. Sometimes

d. Rarely

e. Never

9. When I feel anxious about starting a task, I find myself taking on other projects instead.

a. Always

b. Often

c. Sometimes

d. Rarely

e. Never

10. If I am worried about a task on my plate, I try to keep busy and distract myself.

a. Always

b. Often

c. Sometimes

d. Rarely

e. Never

## DISENGAGEMENT

1. When I have a long to-do list, the first thing I want to do is take a nap.

a. Always

b. Often

c. Sometimes

d. Rarely

e. Never

2. I find myself on social media, websites, or apps when I should be doing other things.

   a. Always

   b. Often

   c. Sometimes

   d. Rarely

   e. Never

3. When I am overwhelmed, I tend to zone out.

   a. Always

   b. Often

   c. Sometimes

   d. Rarely

   e. Never

4. When I have a new task, I will do anything to turn my brain off and not think about it.

   a. Always

   b. Often

   c. Sometimes

   d. Rarely

   e. Never

5. When I feel stressed about my responsibilities, I tend to use downer drugs and alcohol.

   a. Always

   b. Often

   c. Sometimes

   d. Rarely

   e. Never

6. Sometimes I just can't get going on a new project, even

when it's important.

a. Always

b. Often

c. Sometimes

d. Rarely

e. Never

7. I find myself binge-watching television even when I have responsibilities to handle.

a. Always

b. Often

c. Sometimes

d. Rarely

e. Never

8. I often want to give up on my goals when I feel frustrated or overwhelmed.

a. Always

b. Often

c. Sometimes

d. Rarely

e. Never

9. When I have a pressing task, I find myself daydreaming about other things I wish to do.

a. Always

b. Often

c. Sometimes

d. Rarely

e. Never

10. When I am feeling overwhelmed, I tend to go into my

shell.

a. Always

b. Often

c. Sometimes

d. Rarely

e. Never

**Scoring**

Mobilization                          Disengagement

A _____ x 5 = _____                   A _____ x 5 = _____

B _____ x 4 = _____                   B _____ x 4 = _____

C _____ x 3 = _____                   C _____ x 3 = _____

D _____ x 2 = _____                   D _____ x 2 = _____

E _____ x 1 = _____                   E _____ x 1 = _____

TOTAL = _____                         TOTAL = _____

## Scoring[3]

### 42 – 50 = Very High

A very high score means your body really does not like handling tasks that spark anxiety. It's great that you're here, so you can learn to support your system like it needs to be supported.

If you mobilize, you may find yourself extremely busy around final exam time doing everything except studying. Or you may over-study to the point of exhaustion. Obviously, neither of these two options are going to help your exam score.

If you disengage, you may be all caught up on the last five seasons of your favorite television show, but struggle to focus on what is most important.

Remember, no matter what your response, it is your system's way of trying to protect you from something that feels scary. While that exam or work presentation isn't a saber-toothed tiger, your body doesn't necessarily know that.

If you score high in both mobilization and disengagement, your reaction may vary depending upon the task or situation.

---

3   Task Approach is a new concept developed for this book. Existing research was consulted in the following areas of study, with selected citations noted: procrastination (Becker and Cropanzano, 2010; Steel, 2007), emotional dysregulation (Amali, Chowdhury and Pychyl, 2017; Eckert et al., 2016; Leith and Baumeister, 1996; Sirois and Giguere, 2018), vagal tone (Beauchine, 2001; Beauchaine, Gatzke-Kopp and Mead, 2007; Rash and Aguierre-Camacho, 2012), psychological flexibility (Glick, Millstein and Orsillo, 2014) and Reinforcement Sensitivity Theory (Corr and Cooper, 2016). All items were newly created specifically for this inventory.

Once you bring your system into a state of greater equilibrium you will be able to handle life's challenges much more easily.

### 34 – 41 = High

A high score means your nervous system could use a hand. That's okay because we all need help sometimes, don't we?

As a mobilizer, you might stay up too late double checking your work spreadsheet or starting a new craft project, despite the fact that your presentation is due in the morning.

If you disengage, you might spend more time than you mean to absent-mindedly scrolling through your phone, unable to find the energy necessary to get up and get working.

When you return to your center, where your true power lies, you will be able to focus as necessary in a healthy, balanced way.

### 26-33 = Medium

A medium score means that you struggle with task approach to some degree. Awareness is the first step to change, and by taking this inventory you're already on your way.

You may only find yourself going into mobilization or disengagement at certain times or under specific situations. Applaud yourself for the times you *do* approach your to-do list in a healthy, head-on fashion, and have compassion for yourself in the times you simply cannot. By allowing yourself to mess up, you also give yourself an opportunity to observe just how your system is reacting.

## 18-25 = Low

A low score means this form of task anxiety is only occasionally a problem for you, or that it is of low intensity when it does happen. You may be annoyed by yourself at times, but still manage to get most of your important tasks completed, even if they're not fun.

Pay attention to when you do find yourself in mobilization or disengagement and the circumstances surrounding it. The more you are aware of your patterns, the more you will be able to begin interrupting your procrastinating behavior. In time, they might cease to exist altogether!

## 10-17 = Very Low

A very low score indicates this type of task approach is not very relevant in your life. If you have a higher score on the opposite form of task approach, then your pattern is quite clear.

However, if both your scores are low or very low, congratulations! You have either done a great deal of work to get here, or you are fortunate to have a healthy approach to completing the tasks in your life.

## ASSESSMENT # 3: ORGANIZATIONAL STYLE

An individual with a well-functioning nervous system regularly experiences a sense of confidence, coherence, flexibility, and is resilient in the face of stress or challenge. Organizational style is a measure of the nervous system's tendency to operate outside of this happy homeostasis, due to unprocessed trauma remaining in the body.

The healthy zone for the nervous system operates primarily within a window of tolerance (as described by Ogden, Minton, and Pain, 2006), where one can tolerate occasional dips out of this range. However, a disorganized nervous system frequently functions above or below this window, with too much (hyperarousal) or too little (hypoarousal) activation. Hyperarousal, also known as fragmentation, involves activation of the sympathetic branch of the nervous system (flight-or-fight) and results in a fragmentation of the system, in which the individual has difficulty managing overwhelming emotions or racing thoughts, and may feel on guard. Hypoarousal, also known as rigidity, involves activation of the dorsal vagal branch of the vagus nerve and results in a sense of rigidity within the system, in which one tends toward emotional numbness, rigid thoughts and behaviors, as well as dissociation.

Each extreme comes with specific physical, mental, emotional, and behavioral tendencies. Anyone can experience this nervous system dysregulation sometimes; however, with unprocessed trauma, one may either remain stuck in this place or return too easily to either extreme. Some individuals bounce between the two. Understanding your organizational style can help you identify areas in which you are struggling that you may not realize are due to the state of your nervous system. Completing exercises tailored to your particular system may help you move toward a sense of inner peace, confidence, and harmony.

### RIGIDITY

1. I follow a strict daily routine and feel upset when things don't go as planned.
   a. Always
   b. Often
   c. Sometimes
   d. Rarely
   e. Never
2. I find it difficult to change my way of doing something even though it may not be successful.
   a. Always
   b. Often
   c. Sometimes
   d. Rarely
   e. Never
3. I find myself doing things I *should* be doing instead of things I *want* to be doing.

a. Always

b. Often

c. Sometimes

d. Rarely

e. Never

4. I cannot tolerate it when things are out of order or disorganized.

   a. Always

   b. Often

   c. Sometimes

   d. Rarely

   e. Never

5. There are times when I feel like my eyes cannot focus
   clearly around me.

   a. Always

   b. Often

   c. Sometimes

   d. Rarely

   e. Never

6. I tend to get diarrhea.

   a. Always

   b. Often

   c. Sometimes

   d. Rarely

   e. Never

7. I tend to feel more fatigued than energized.

   a. Always

   b. Often

c. Sometimes

d. Rarely

e. Never

8. There are times when I can't get moving, even though I want to.

   a. Always

   b. Often

   c. Sometimes

   d. Rarely

   e. Never

9. When I am somewhere I don't want to be, I mentally take myself elsewhere.

   a. Always

   b. Often

   c. Sometimes

   d. Rarely

   e. Never

10. I feel like I am in a fog and things around me seem unreal.

    a. Always

    b. Often

    c. Sometimes

    d. Rarely

    e. Never

11. My opinions are fairly stable and rarely change.

    a. Always

    b. Often

    c. Sometimes

    d. Rarely

e. Never

12. My thinking is very black and white; it's difficult for me to find a gray area.
    a. Always
    b. Often
    c. Sometimes
    d. Rarely
    e. Never

13. I often do not feel emotionally connected to situations around me.
    a. Always
    b. Often
    c. Sometimes
    d. Rarely
    e. Never

14. I have a difficult time crying when I feel sad. The tears do not seem to come.
    a. Always
    b. Often
    c. Sometimes
    d. Rarely
    e. Never

15. Sometimes I feel like a robot instead of a person.
    a. Always
    b. Often
    c. Sometimes
    d. Rarely
    e. Never

16. I feel hopeless, helpless, and like a victim.

    a. Always

    b. Often

    c. Sometimes

    d. Rarely

    e. Never

## FRAGMENTATION

1.  I tend to lose things.

    a. Always

    b. Often

    c. Sometimes

    d. Rarely

    e. Never

2.  I start multiple projects at the same time and tend not to finish many.

    a. Always

    b. Often

    c. Sometimes

    d. Rarely

    e. Never

3.  I find it difficult to follow directions or instructions.

    a. Always

    b. Often

    c. Sometimes

    d. Rarely

    e. Never

4.  I find it hard to stay disciplined and keep a regular rou-

tine.

a. Always

b. Often

c. Sometimes

d. Rarely

e. Never

5. I have difficulty falling or staying asleep.

a. Always

b. Often

c. Sometimes

d. Rarely

e. Never

6. I tend to get constipated.

a. Always

b. Often

c. Sometimes

d. Rarely

e. Never

7. I notice that I have a hard time sitting still when I have a lot on my mind.

a. Always

b. Often

c. Sometimes

d. Rarely

e. Never

8. There are times when I feel like my mouth is dry and I can't quench my thirst.

a. Always

b. Often

c. Sometimes

d. Rarely

e. Never

9. My mind thinks about certain thoughts, topics, or events even when I don't want to.

a. Always

b. Often

c. Sometimes

d. Rarely

e. Never

10. When my mind wanders, it's hard to bring myself back into focus.

a. Always

b. Often

c. Sometimes

d. Rarely

e. Never

11. It feels like my mind is constantly analyzing what is happening in my life.

a. Always

b. Often

c. Sometimes

d. Rarely

e. Never

12. My mind is always going, and I have a hard time focusing on one specific thought.

a. Always

b. Often

c. Sometimes

d. Rarely

e. Never

13. I have to be on guard all of the time.

a. Always

b. Often

c. Sometimes

d. Rarely

e. Never

14. I feel people can't be trusted.

a. Always

b. Often

c. Sometimes

d. Rarely

e. Never

15. I am easily agitated.

a. Always

b. Often

c. Sometimes

d. Rarely

e. Never

16. When I'm upset, my emotions feel overwhelming.

a. Always

b. Often

c. Sometimes

d. Rarely

e. Never

## Scoring[4]

| Rigidity | | |
|---|---|---|
| A _____ | x 5 = | _____ |
| B _____ | x 4 = | _____ |
| C _____ | x 3 = | _____ |
| D _____ | x 2 = | _____ |
| E _____ | x 1 = | _____ |
| TOTAL = _____ | | |

| Fragmentation | | |
|---|---|---|
| A _____ | x 5 = | _____ |
| B _____ | x 4 = | _____ |
| C _____ | x 3 = | _____ |
| D _____ | x 2 = | _____ |
| E _____ | x 1 = | _____ |
| TOTAL = _____ | | |

## 68-80 = Very High

A very high score indicates rigidity or fragmentation are very active in your body and life overall.

A very high rigidity score indicates that your nervous system is so shut down, it is as if your mind and body wish to turn into stone. With a strict schedule, recurring thoughts, and

---

4    A number of existing measures in related areas were consulted in the creation of this scale. This scale borrows Q2 from the Wesley Rigidity Scale Short Form (WRS) (Zelen and Levitt, 1954); Q9 from the Adolescent Dissociative Experiences Scale (A-DES) (Armstrong, Putnam, Carlson, Libero, and Smith, 1997); Q10 from the Trauma Symptom Checklist-40 (Brierie and Runtz, 1989); Q27 from the Hyperarousal Scale (HAS) (Hammad, Barsky, and Regestein 2001); Q29 and 30 from the Posttraumatic Cognitions Inventory (PCI) (Foa et al., 1999), Q31 from the Emotional Reactivity Scale (ERS) (Nock et al., 2008), and Q32 from the Multidimensional Assessment of Emotion Regulation and Dysregulation Scale (MAERD) (Gratz and Roemer, 2004). All remaining items were specifically created for this scale

a limited window of emotion, being rigid may quell some anxiety, but it does not necessarily feel good.

A very high fragmentation score means your system is so overwhelmed that you may frequently find yourself in an emotional hurricane. In this state, it can be hard to keep *anything* straight, difficult to maintain a regular schedule, and sleep problems and emotional agitation are the norm.

A very high score in both rigidity and fragmentation shows that your system may be compensating for such a high sense of overwhelm (fragmentation), that it winds up shutting down to the other extreme (rigidity) in an attempt to find relief.

All information is good information to have. The better you understand your patterns, even if they tend toward the extreme, the more empowered you are to take one step, then another, then another, toward a life in which you feel stable, balanced, and at peace.

### 55-67 = High

A high score means that rigidity or fragmentation are pretty serious business for you.

With a high level of rigidity, your daily life is likely marked by regular nervous system dysregulation. You may hate it if someone threw you a surprise birthday party, and be so uncomfortable you couldn't even enjoy the cake.

With a high level of fragmentation, you likely have a difficult time accomplishing many basic goals and tasks, and often become distracted or overwhelmed in the process.

A high score in both rigidity and fragmentation suggests your system bounces back and forth between the two, or that certain situations may trigger a rigid response while others bring up fragmentation.

Everyone is different and will have patterns all over the map. Exercises can help you bring your system into greater alignment with the life you truly want for yourself.

### 39-50 = Medium

A medium score indicates that rigidity or fragmentation may cause you some challenges, but you also spend at least a portion of your time within a healthy window of tolerance. It may be that specific people, places, or situations elicit rigidity or fragmentation in your system, and that those feelings linger longer than you'd like, but not so long you live there 24/7.

If you have been working on yourself for some time, a medium score may be a sign of progress. A rigid individual may feel challenged when plans change at the last minute, or feel unsure how to respond when others cry at a sad movie, yet still be able to tolerate the discomfort.

A fragmented person may frequently lose their keys, arrive late, and have a coffee stain on their shirt, but at least they're still showing up!

Medium scores mean your life is fairly marked by rigidity or fragmentation, but that you can also see the sun shining through.

### 29-41 = Low
A low score suggests that rigidity or fragmentation are a lesser issue in your life. You may find yourself annoyed by some symptoms, but they do not rule your life overall. If one score is low and the other is higher, it indicates the higher score has a greater impact on your life. If both of your scores are low, that means your system is functioning quite healthily, and you only have minor or infrequent occasions of dysregulation.

### 16-28 = Very Low
A very low score means that rigidity or fragmentation are not a pressing concern in your body and, more broadly, in your life.

Pay attention if one of these areas scored higher. If the higher score landed at a medium or above, you may wish to complete relevant exercises to bring your system into a more optimal state. If both of your scores are low or very low, congratulations! Your system is likely functioning within a healthy window. You may find yourself feeling out of whack every once in a blue moon, but it does not appear that nervous system dysregulation is a major problem for you.

## ASSESSMENT #4: THE SENSORY SCALE

The five senses help our nervous system organize and make sense of the world around us. However, when there is a history of trauma, our senses are not always well integrated. This means that individuals might become hypersensitive, rendering what others would consider ordinary sights, sounds, and other senses to become uncomfortable and even overwhelming.

On the other end of the spectrum, people who are hyposensitive fail to notice or register certain senses, creating a lack of awareness and disconnect.

Still, other people experience a combination of hyper- and hyposensitivity, or may be hypersensitive on some senses and hyposensitive on others. This questionnaire will help you understand how your nervous system tends to experience your overall patterns.

## LOW SENSATION

1. I don't notice when someone enters the room.
   a. Always
   b. Often
   c. Sometimes
   d. Rarely
   e. Never

2. When watching sports, I have a difficult time tracking which player has the ball.
   a. Always
   b. Often
   c. Sometimes
   d. Rarely
   e. Never

3. I wouldn't be able to match the color of a sweater in a shop with the color of my pants at home.
   a. Always
   b. Often
   c. Sometimes
   d. Rarely
   e. Never

4. I have difficulty finding people in crowds.
   a. Always
   b. Often
   c. Sometimes
   d. Rarely
   e. Never

5. I can't hear very low frequency sounds, such as low voices or the bass in music.

   a. Always

   b. Often

   c. Sometimes

   d. Rarely

   e. Never

6. I don't pick up on subtleties when someone else is speaking.

   a. Always

   b. Often

   c. Sometimes

   d. Rarely

   e. Never

7. My hearing is fine, but I still often don't notice when someone calls my name.

   a. Always

   b. Often

   c. Sometimes

   d. Rarely

   e. Never

8. I have a hard time distinguishing the words in songs.

   a. Always

   b. Often

   c. Sometimes

   d. Rarely

   e. Never

9. I don't feel it when someone touches me.

a. Always

b. Often

c. Sometimes

d. Rarely

e. Never

10. I have a very high tolerance for pain.

a. Always

b. Often

c. Sometimes

d. Rarely

e. Never

11. I don't seem to notice when my hands or face are dirty.

a. Always

b. Often

c. Sometimes

d. Rarely

e. Never

12. I find cuts and bruises on my body, but don't remember hurting myself.

a. Always

b. Often

c. Sometimes

d. Rarely

e. Never

13. Strong flavors and spicy foods don't bother me.

a. Always

b. Often

c. Sometimes

d. Rarely

e. Never

14. I wouldn't be able to tell the difference in the taste between two different types of apples.

a. Always

b. Often

c. Sometimes

d. Rarely

e. Never

15. I wouldn't taste it if someone added a teaspoon of salt to my glass of water.

a. Always

b. Often

c. Sometimes

d. Rarely

e. Never

16. I have accidentally consumed dairy products that have gone bad because I did not notice.

a. Always

b. Often

c. Sometimes

d. Rarely

e. Never

17. I would be the last person to detect it if something was burning.

a. Always

b. Often

c. Sometimes

d. Rarely

e. Never

18. I can't distinguish a familiar person from a stranger based on their smell.

a. Always

b. Often

c. Sometimes

d. Rarely

e. Never

19. I am unaware of odors that others notice.

a. Always

b. Often

c. Sometimes

d. Rarely

e. Never

20. I can't tell if my clothes are clean or dirty by smell alone.

a. Always

b. Often

c. Sometimes

d. Rarely

e. Never

## HIGH SENSATION

1. Bright lights bother me.

a. Always

b. Often

c. Sometimes

d. Rarely

e. Never

2. I need sunglasses even when it is cloudy outside.

   a. Always

   b. Often

   c. Sometimes

   d. Rarely

   e. Never

3. I am uncomfortable with intense visual scenes, like wild parties, disaster zones, or chaotic scenes in a movie.

   a. Always

   b. Often

   c. Sometimes

   d. Rarely

   e. Never

4. I cannot work in a coffee shop because seeing all of the activity around me is distracting.

   a. Always

   b. Often

   c. Sometimes

   d. Rarely

   e. Never

5. When others are watching television, I either leave the room or ask them to turn it down.

   a. Always

   b. Often

   c. Sometimes

   d. Rarely

   e. Never

6. The sound of others eating can be irritating.

   a. Always

   b. Often

   c. Sometimes

   d. Rarely

   e. Never

7. I find it difficult to work with background noise.

   a. Always

   b. Often

   c. Sometimes

   d. Rarely

   e. Never

8. Unexpected sounds such as sirens or car alarms put me on edge.

   a. Always

   b. Often

   c. Sometimes

   d. Rarely

   e. Never

9. Certain elements of clothing, such as seams, labels, fabric textures, and jewelry irritate me.

   a. Always

   b. Often

   c. Sometimes

   d. Rarely

   e. Never

10. I feel uncomfortable when others touch me, such as during haircuts and visits to the doctor.

a. Always

b. Often

c. Sometimes

d. Rarely

e. Never

11. I don't like it when I have to stand too close to other people in line.

a. Always

b. Often

c. Sometimes

d. Rarely

e. Never

12. I avoid going barefoot in the dirt or sand.

a. Always

b. Often

c. Sometimes

d. Rarely

e. Never

13. I don't like strong-tasting mints or candies.

a. Always

b. Often

c. Sometimes

d. Rarely

e. Never

14. I am sensitive to the texture of food.

a. Always

b. Often

c. Sometimes

d. Rarely

e. Never

15. I always buy the same brands of food. If the store is out of what I like, I cannot tolerate the alternative.

a. Always

b. Often

c. Sometimes

d. Rarely

e. Never

16. I sense that food has gone bad and cannot eat it before others do.

a. Always

b. Often

c. Sometimes

d. Rarely

e. Never

17. I am hypersensitive to strong smells.

a. Always

b. Often

c. Sometimes

d. Rarely

e. Never

18. I become overwhelmed by the scent of other people's deodorant, shampoo, or soap.

a. Always

b. Often

c. Sometimes

d. Rarely

e. Never

19. I react strongly to smells that don't seem to bother others.

   a. Always

   b. Often

   c. Sometimes

   d. Rarely

   e. Never

20. I will not eat a food that smells strange.

   a. Always

   b. Often

   c. Sometimes

   d. Rarely

   e. Never

## Scoring[5]

| Low Sensation | High Sensation |
|---|---|
| A _____ x 5 = _____ | A _____ x 5 = _____ |
| B _____ x 4 = _____ | B _____ x 4 = _____ |
| C _____ x 3 = _____ | C _____ x 3 = _____ |

---

5   A number of existing measures for sensory processing were consulted to create this scale. This scale borrows Q3, 5, 15, 17, 18, 20, 24, 35, and 37 from the Sensory Perception Quotient (SPQ) (Tavassoli et al., 2014) and Q11, 19, 27, 33, and 40 from the Adult Sensory Profile (ASP) (Brown et al., 2001). In addition, Q23 was edited from the Highly Sensitive Person Scale (HSPS) (Aaron and Aaron, 1997) and Q32 was edited from the Short Sensory Profile (Tomcheck and Dunn, 2007). All remaining items were created specifically for this scale.

D _____ x 2 = _____          D _____ x 2 = _____

E _____ x 1 = _____          E _____ x 1 = _____

TOTAL = _____                TOTAL = _____


## Scoring

## 84-100 = Very High

A very high score indicates that your nervous system is poorly attuned to your senses. But, remember! Knowledge is power.

If you are hypersensitive, you may feel as if someone has turned the volume on your senses all the way up, which can make navigating life very uncomfortable. This may affect your daily routine or cause you to feel the desire to avoid certain people, places, or situations.

If you are hyposensitive, a lack of awareness may cause you to feel as if the volume is so low you can't even tell there is music playing. Disengaged from the world around you, you may miss important cues that are obvious to others.

A very high score may appear alarming, but there is no need to fear; it only means there is tremendous potential for improvement.

### 67-83 = High

A high score means that your body tends toward either hyper- or hypoarousal. Your nervous system is not properly processing your senses. For hypersensitive individuals, this might mean that the hot tub is scalding; for hyposensitive folks, the water is just getting warm enough.

Addressing your senses will help turn your body's reaction up or down, to a more pleasant sense of equilibrium.

### 50-66 = Medium

This range indicates that you may have some issues with your senses.

On the hypersensitive end, your senses may bother you, though they are not debilitating. You can still get by. Some might use strategies to minimize their discomfort, like bringing ear plugs to the computer lab if other users' typing is obnoxious to them.

On the hyposensitive end, having lesser awareness of these senses may create some feeling of disconnect from the world around you, but you have enough presence to generally feel okay. You may need the television turned up higher than your spouse would like, but not so loud that you drive your partner out of the room.

Overall, your system experiences some hyper- or hyposensitivity, but it doesn't prevent you from participating in everyday life activities.

### 33-49 = Low

A low score means your nervous system responds relatively appropriately to its senses. When hypersensitivity does arise, it is more annoying than it is panic inducing. Hyposensitive people are a little numbed out, but still present enough to get with the program.

### 20-32 = Very Low

A very low score suggests your nervous system may have few or no problems processing your senses and they don't cause you any extra stress. Even if the tag in the back of your shirt is a little scratchy now and then, you feel no sense of alarm at all.

A very low hyposensitive score indicates you have enough awareness of your senses that they do not seem to cause major problems. You're never in danger of burning the house down, even if it occasionally takes you a second longer than your family members to notice food burning on the stove.

## ASSESSMENT #5: INTEROCEPTION

Interoception is the ability to sense the inner state of your body. We receive internal signals (which some refer to as a sixth sense) that manifest in sensations like a gut feeling. The greater our inner awareness and the better we understand how we feel, the more power we have to handle life's challenges and to make positive choices.

When trauma is present, a person's interoceptive ability is reduced because past traumatic energy remains active inside the body, resulting in various physical, mental, and emotional discomforts. Many people who suffer from trauma learn to numb these uncomfortable sensations as a means of protecting themselves. The discomfort, overwhelm, and subsequent numbing unintentionally deaden a person's inner awareness, which also serves as the source of their power.

Interoception is a skill that can be improved, both in terms of increasing awareness and increasing accuracy of what is sensed.

## INTEROCEPTION

1. When I am tense, I can determine where the tension is located in my body.
   a. Always
   b. Often
   c. Sometimes
   d. Rarely
   e. Never
2. I notice when I am uncomfortable in my body.

a. Always

b. Often

c. Sometimes

d. Rarely

e. Never

3. I try to address and alleviate sensations of discomfort.

   a. Always

   b. Often

   c. Sometimes

   d. Rarely

   e. Never

4. I try not to distract myself from what I sense even when I experience unpleasant physical sensations.

   a. Always

   b. Often

   c. Sometimes

   d. Rarely

   e. Never

5. I am attuned to when something does not feel right in my body.

   a. Always

   b. Often

   c. Sometimes

   d. Rarely

   e. Never

6. I can distinguish between pleasant and unpleasant sensations in my body.

   a. Always

b. Often

c. Sometimes

d. Rarely

e. Never

7.  I can pay attention to my breath without being distracted by things happening around me.

    a. Always

    b. Often

    c. Sometimes

    d. Rarely

    e. Never

8.  I can pay attention to my posture while also having a conversation with someone.

    a. Always

    b. Often

    c. Sometimes

    d. Rarely

    e. Never

9.  When something is wrong in my life, I can feel it in my body.

    a. Always

    b. Often

    c. Sometimes

    d. Rarely

    e. Never

10. I notice how my body changes when I feel happy or joyful.

    a. Always

b. Often

c. Sometimes

d. Rarely

e. Never

11. When I bring awareness to my body, I feel a sense of calm.

a. Always

b. Often

c. Sometimes

d. Rarely

e. Never

12. When I am caught up in my thoughts, I can calm my mind by focusing on my body or breath.

a. Always

b. Often

c. Sometimes

d. Rarely

e. Never

13. I listen to my body for information about my emotional state.

a. Always

b. Often

c. Sometimes

d. Rarely

e. Never

14. When I am upset, I take time to explore how my body feels.

a. Always

b. Often

c. Sometimes

d. Rarely

e. Never

15. I feel my body is a safe place.

a. Always

b. Often

c. Sometimes

d. Rarely

e. Never

16. I trust my body sensations.

a. Always

b. Often

c. Sometimes

d. Rarely

e. Never

## Scoring[6]

A _____ x 5 = _____

B _____ x 4 = _____

C _____ x 3 = _____

---

6   This scale was adapted from the Multidimensional Assessment of Interoceptive Awareness, Version 2 (MAIA-2) (Mehling 2018). In addition, existing research and writing was consulted in the creation of this scale. Selected citations include Craig, 2003; Ceunen, Vlaaien and Van Diest, 2016; Damasio, 2003; Harshaw, 2015; Ma-Kellams, 2014; Mehling, 2016; Ogden, Minton and Pain, 2006; Porges, 2011; and van der Kolk 2014.

D _____ x 2 = _____

E _____ x 1 = _____

TOTAL = _____

### 68-80 = Very High

A very high score makes you akin to an interoceptive wizard, peering deep into your inner world with a crystal ball. You are comfortable noticing and being present with whatever happens in your body, whether it feels pleasant or unpleasant. Your greatest power lies in your ability to surf the waves of life—even through the rough storms—while remaining centered and true to yourself. By all means, continue to enjoy the deep relationship you have cultivated with your body and spirit.

### 55-67 = High

With a high interoception score, you are like a great yoga master who is typically in tune with their mind, body, spirit, and nature. Occasionally, you might slip into that human place of confusion and disconnect but, overall, your interoceptive capacity is excellent and you can generally handle it when it falters.

### 42-54 = Medium

A medium score means that your interoceptive skills are a bit hit or miss. Imagine a psychic who foretells a few pieces of your future with eerie accuracy, yet somehow also ignores the bright pink elephant in the room. You have a relationship with your inner world, and sometimes you are very in tune; other times, all you sense is static. Perhaps you sometimes ignore your inner voice, only to later realize, "I *knew* that was going to happen!" Celebrate when you can be present and trust your body, and have empathy for the times you are disconnected. Enhancing your interoception may help you nurture and expand your capacity to listen deeply.

### 29-41 = Low

If you score low on interoception, the image of a floating head might be an apt depiction of your inner experience. A mind severed from its body will not be able to hear very well. Unfortunately, your body has many things to say, yet you are likely not hearing them, so many other aspects of your life may feel off. Remember, this is not your fault; it's simply the way your body has responded to past trauma. Practicing interoception should help you begin to notice sensations and emotions in your body, be more present, and ultimately lead you to a place where you can use your body and breath for self-soothing.

### 16-28 = Very Low

A very low interoception score indicates great room for improvement and an exciting adventure ahead. Many people are quite disconnected from their bodies these days. In a culture that celebrates mind over matter, you are far from alone. As you continue up the stairway toward increased interoception, life will become more vivid and you will feel a deeper connection to your body and self. You may encounter sensations that are uncomfortable as well, but that is still progress. Learning to simply be with these feelings is the same skill that allows us to be with our happiness and joy. Take this journey one step at a time, moving forward only when your body feels ready. In time, you will likely feel more centered and connected than ever before.

# CHAPTER SIX

---

# HEALING EXERCISES

The purpose of the following exercises is to inspire you to get curious about yourself. It's about starting to connect with and develop a deeper relationship with yourself—a relationship based on an awareness of your senses and physical being. I want you to discover the survival energy in your body. I want you to learn what feels good and what doesn't, to observe which exercises feel more fluid and which ones feel like a chore.

I advise you to try out one exercise at a time as appropriate, rather than attempting to do them all at once. Take your time. Along the way, you will develop a greater awareness about how your nervous system functions. As you begin incorporating these exercises into your healing routine, give yourself a couple of weeks before you decide how you feel about them. The slower you go, the faster you'll make progress. Set yourself up for success by building a sense of mastery instead of frustration. With this in mind, a gentle approach is always better.

To determine where to start, we will refer back to your assessments in the previous chapter. You will begin with exercises that address the areas where you scored in the highest range (in other words, in the very high and high range) and work your way forward from there. You will also notice that I have included a couple of advanced exercises at the end of the book. You should practice these only after you have built up a sense of confidence and mastery in the earlier exercises.

### BREATH WORK EXERCISE

*This is a great exercise for everyone, no matter where you scored on each individual assessment.*

Our primary goal is to regulate and balance our nervous system, and this is a tool we can all use at any time in order to do this. This type of regulated breath work helps manage stress of all levels and varieties and brings us back to the present moment.

We know that breath work is good for your heart rate variability, which is how the nervous system is regulated.

High heart rate variability contributes to a balanced autonomic nervous system.

Begin this exercise by lying down on the ground. Notice how laying directly on the floor provides a sensation of being grounded to the earth. Place one hand on your heart and the other on your stomach. Inhale deeply through your nose as you silently count to three. Exhale all of the air out through your mouth as you silently count to six. Repeat this six times, and then see if you can add on time, inhaling as you count to four, and exhaling as you count to eight. Do this for another six rounds of breath, then see if you can work up to a five-count inhale, followed by a ten-count exhale.

Once you are up and moving around, notice if you feel calmer. Do you feel more present? In what ways do you feel different now than you did when you started?

## ORIENTING EXERCISE

*Start here if you scored very high or high on the fight, flight, or freeze assessment.*

This exercise will help you practice using your five senses and is a great tool for increasing nervous system regulation. It will help you begin to more accurately sense whether or not you need to use your survival instincts of fight, flight, or freeze.

Animals in the wild are constantly scanning their environment to make sure they are safe. Likewise, this exercise is about connecting to where you are and creating awareness of your environment. When people experience a lot of trauma, they tend to either view their environment as a danger or to disassociate from it. To build a sense of safety, it helps to notice the entrances and exits, as well as particular visual elements or smells in your environment. This exercise will help you start to pay attention to what's around you instead of disconnecting from it.

Begin this exercise by taking note of how you feel, both physically and emotionally.

Now, look around the room. Turn your head in all directions and notice where the entry to the room is. Now notice what it feels like to be supported by the chair or floor. Spend about one minute scanning the room for objects, colors, and shapes.

Now, start to connect with your other senses. What smells do you notice? What do you hear? Is there a taste in your mouth—including the taste of nothing?

Check in with yourself again, noticing how you feel both physically and emotionally. What, if anything, has changed since you began this exercise?

## SURVIVAL ENERGY EXERCISE

*Start here if you scored very high or high on the fight, flight, or freeze or interoception assessments.*

When unresolved trauma energy becomes locked in the body, it is often a result of feeling as though we weren't in charge of or able to defend ourselves from danger, either emotionally or physically, in the past. This exercise will help you generate and access energy that is stored in your body from a time or times in the past when you didn't feel safe. It will unlock that energy and assist you in releasing trauma and restoring equilibrium.

This exercise is ideally performed with a partner. I recommend you do it with a trusted person who feels safe to you. If that is not possible, instead perform the first part of this exercise on your own, pushing against a wall.

Have your partner brace themselves against a wall as you push against their hands for between ten and sixty seconds, then stop. Release your partner, close your eyes, and tune into your body. How is it reacting? What physical sensations do you feel? How about emotional? Repeat this pushing and checking in two or three times. Notice if the sensations remain the same or change.

Now trade places so that the other person is pushing you. Again, check in after each interval. Notice your sensations and feelings. How do you feel being pushed as compared to when you were pushing? Note if your reaction changes in any way from one interval to the next.

## RESOURCING EXERCISE

*Start here if you scored very high or high on the task approach or organization assessments.*

In this exercise, we are going to build a resource list. This is a list of internal and external resources you have at your disposal. A resource can be any person, place, or thing that makes you feel safe. An external resource might be as wide-ranging as a dog, a close friend, or even a pillow. It might be your job or a specific location. Maybe it's your favorite hiking trail.

An internal resource is something inside of you, something you know about yourself. For example, my best internal resource is my ability to connect with people. Another is my ability to maintain a good attitude when shit hits the fan.

To figure out your own resources, start paying attention to the moments when you feel the strongest and most in charge. What makes you feel accomplished and confident? Think back to a time in your life when you encountered a difficult experience and dissect some of the things that helped you through that. You can also ask a safe person who knows you well for their input.

It is important to understand what the resources in your life are so that, in moments when you require them, you can go directly to them. Aside from that, just thinking about our resources can produce more feel-good hormones and less stress hormones. Using our resources is how we build resilience, and resilience is how we build a sense of mastery to know that we can handle the stress in our life.

Make a practice of writing down five internal and five external resources. Keep this list on your phone or in a journal and continue adding to it. Read this list every morning when you get up and every evening before you go to sleep as a reminder to yourself that you have resources at your disposal when you need them.

## SENSING EXERCISE

*Start here if you scored very high or high on the sensory or interoception assessments.*

This exercise is designed to help you build your own sensory toolbox. A sensory toolbox is a collection of sensory strategies that will help build and support a healthy sensory system. When trauma strikes, we often lose our ability to accurately sense how we feel inside our bodies and in the world. The goal of this exercise is to discover tools that will help you connect more deeply to your interoceptive and proprioceptive systems. Ultimately, it will help you connect to your emotional states in a more present and objective manner. To do this, you will safely explore your senses and get curious about which sensations feel comfortable to you. This is an important step in helping your central nervous system process sensory information from your body and respond to it accurately.

To begin, use your instincts to decide which sense you want to explore first. If you are uncertain how to do this, simply get curious about what feels good to you.

### SMELL

Start by discovering the different and distinct smells of essential oils. If you find a smell that you connect with, put it in your toolbox. You may want to carry this essential oil around with you and take it out a few times a day, especially during those moments when you find it difficult to stay present.

### TOUCH

Begin to discover what different textures feel like against your skin. I invite you to visit a fabric store and take yourself on a tactile journey, exploring the different textures and shapes. Once you have discovered a few textures that feel calming to your system, put them in your toolbox. Perhaps you keep a piece of this fabric in your pocket and touch it when you feel anxious.

### SIGHT

We all ground differently in our senses, and some of us ground through our visual sense. I invite you to go to a museum, look at art books, look at pictures, notice the colors, and notice what thoughts and feelings come up for you as you observe. Get curious about what shapes and colors appeal to you. Do you notice any patterns?

Or, perhaps you simply like the more general visual landscape of nature. Go outside and look around. Notice how different scenery makes you feel.

If you notice that particular sights are soothing to you, keep a picture of that sight either on your phone or printed out and readily available. Or, if you prefer to see certain sights in person, perhaps try stepping outside or taking yourself on a walk the next time your nervous system needs some TLC.

## SOUND

Pay attention to which sounds and genres of music feel comfortable to you. Or perhaps you notice that being outside and listening to the sounds of birds tweeting or water running is calming and peaceful for you. Once you have determined what feels relaxing, put together a playlist or take note of the sounds that will nourish your system each day. Spend a few minutes with these sounds daily.

## TASTE

I do not recommend using taste as a dominant tool (especially if you have a history of or are currently dealing with disordered eating). While we all have our comfort foods that can calm and regulate our nervous system, using taste as a soothing mechanism includes many complexities that go beyond the scope of this book.

Use the information you gleaned from this exercise to identify some new tools you can use when you find yourself in a moment of feeling overwhelmed, dysregulated, or disoriented. Write down or keep with you the scents, textures, sights, and sounds that soothe you in a place that you can easily access. When you find yourself in need of calm or soothing, you can redirect your senses to those things that calm your system. Even better, you can begin to build resiliency in your nervous system by calling upon these senses on a regular basis as a way of keeping your nervous system regulated on an ongoing basis.

## SELF-SOOTHING EXERCISE

*Start here if you scored very high or high on the interoception assessment.*

This exercise is designed to help calm the nervous system and begin to build boundaries and safety in the body. Physical and emotional boundaries go hand and hand and help us form a distinct identity. Boundaries also help us protect ourselves and define what is acceptable.

Set a timer for five minutes and notice how you feel at the end of that time period. If five minutes feels like too much, see if you can start with three minutes and build from there.

Put on some gentle music, something melodic so that you can connect with the sound.

Wrap your arms around yourself and hold the safe container of your body. See what it feels like. What do you notice when you hold yourself?

Rub your palms together. Notice the heat, energy, and friction being created in your body. Now, rub the bottoms of your feet together and, again, notice the heat, energy, and friction.

Place one hand on your stomach and the other hand on your heart. If it feels comfortable to you, close your eyes. Feel your breath rise and fall as you listen to the music. Observe any sensation you might be feeling in your body. Do you feel your heart beating? Do you feel the movement of your stomach? Just notice and see if you can release all judgment and, instead, sit with the sensations.

## ADVANCED EXERCISES
### BOUNDARY EXERCISE

*This is an advanced exercise that should be done after you have explored and mastered all of the other exercises in this chapter. It is especially helpful if your scores on the fight, flight, or freeze or interoception assessments are very high or high.*

This is a more advanced exercise, and requires another person. Your partner should be someone who feels safe to you. The purpose here is to create internal awareness of your body and the messages it sends you, as well as to observe how you feel in time and space with another human being. It should be done in silence in order for you to stay out of a story and, instead, to drop deeper into your body.

Stand in a room at a distance from your partner. You

should be far enough away from your partner that you feel safe and in command of your own space. Begin slowly walking toward your partner. As you move closer, observe what it feels like when the other person doesn't move, what it feels like to get close to them, what it feels like to make eye contact without speaking. Notice how you feel in relationship to another human being.

If you feel triggered in any way, use your voice to say you're uncomfortable. Stop the exercise and revisit it another time. When you feel safe and comfortable, try again, observing whether or not the practice becomes more or less comfortable on different days with the same person.

Ideally, you will start building greater resilience as you gain clarity on where and when you feel threatened. Maybe you will come to realize, "This is a safe person. I know I'm safe, but my internal state is telling me something else." Over time, you should become more able to tolerate it. As you revisit this exercise, notice if you can begin to stay with it for longer amounts of time, even if you are only increasing that amount of time by a few seconds.

FREE-FLOW DANCE EXERCISE

*This is an advanced exercise that should be done after you have explored and mastered all of the other exercises in this chapter. It is especially helpful if your scores on the task and organization assessments are very high or high.*

I love this exercise because it will help you sense your body in time and space and to let go of all the stories you may be telling yourself about your body. Over time, you might even get to a point where you may want to try this exercise unclothed.

This exercise is about giving yourself the space and permission to experience spontaneous body movements. Our body develops a kind of inflexibility and rigidity in response to trauma, which prevents us from moving fluidly. This exercise is intended to bring you back to the embryonic fluid, where you moved with ease and freedom.

Do this exercise in the privacy of your own space, somewhere that you feel comfortable, and put on whatever music you like. I recommend music that will inspire you to move with freedom. Start with three minutes of free-flowing movement. Eventually, work your way up to ten minutes.

Observe how you feel both before and after. Does your body feel more joyful or more fatigued? How about your energy levels? Are they higher or lower? What do you feel compelled to do after you finish moving? Is there greater mobilization in your body, or do you feel like you want to collapse? Does free-flow dance build your confidence, or does it make you feel more anxious or depressed?

## YOU'VE TAKEN A BIG STEP FORWARD

Congratulations on putting focused energy into healing your nervous system! At first you may not feel these shifts, but practicing these exercises on a regular basis are much like building a muscle in the more physical sense. At first, the changes are subtle—so much so that you might not even notice anything has changed. Then, over time, you will discover you have strength that you never did before. You will build muscle memory. Things that previously seemed impossible are all of a sudden abundantly accessible to you.

# CHAPTER SEVEN

---

# LIVING A
# HEALING
# LIFESTYLE

When we are in pain and suffering, we want to find relief, a way out. Here's the thing, though: for as counterintuitive as it may feel, what we really need to find is a way *into* our psychological pain. The more we try to escape the pain, the worse we make it. We are not allowing ourselves to move through the grief, loss, fear, or whatever else it is that needs to be processed and integrated into our nervous system.

Just think about what happens when you push against a heavy object as opposed to leaning into it. When we push, we only get more resistance. It will push back. However, when we allow ourselves to instead lean in, we can relax, exert less effort, and experience far less resistance.

Healing is not a one-and-done process. True, deep, and lasting healing is about making a choice to expand our capacity to evolve and elevate ourselves to the next level of being. We have to decide to get to the next level of connecting to ourselves, connecting to others, and connecting to the world. It is through this process of connection that we can experience deeper and more meaningful relationships in a safe and healthy way. To do this, we have to build up layers of resilience and an understanding of the resources we have at our disposal. These layers include building a sense of safety, attuning to ourselves, and getting to the point where we can attend to building and maintaining our relationships in a healthy way.

As we create our own unique healing lifestyle, we're going for small victories. Like diets, there is no such thing as a sustainable quick fix. This is an ongoing pursuit because we are going to have adversity in our lives; however, we also have the ongoing opportunity to build resilience in ourselves. Each small victory in the midst of life's adversity builds resilience, and resilience builds safety. It provides us with the knowledge that, no matter what happens, we are going to be okay. It is because of this build-up of resilience that I was able to make it through when my husband died. I had already shown myself that I had the amazing ability to stand up in the face of adversity. I knew that, even though I was scared and incredibly heartbroken, I was strong. Because of this, I could tolerate what was in front of me at that moment, even though I didn't like it. I understood that what made me resilient was my own unique resources, which included the ability to connect with myself and those around me. So I kept on doing that, even when I really didn't want to. It was a practice.

There are a million different ways to heal and create resiliency, but the body has to be part of this process. For some people, that will mean moving in an intentional way. For others it will mean establishing a greater connection to their sensory experiences. For many, it will be a combination of these two things. Our body is the vehicle toward holistic healing. Through our body, we can heal the parts of the brain where trauma resides; it is how we can speak the sensory language of trauma.

As you move through the tips for creating a healing lifestyle in this chapter, notice if you feel overwhelmed. If an idea feels like too much right now, that's totally okay. In fact, that's a great reaction to notice. Feel free to skip over that suggestion and move on to something that feels more manageable. Later on, after you've built up more resources and resiliency, you might find that what initially seemed insurmountable now feels possible. Each of these shifts should feel organic and manageable as you build your way up to them one small step at a time.

Anything that doesn't feel that way isn't going to stick over the long haul.

## BECOME YOUR OWN OBSERVER

As you begin to move away from the quick-fix box, the first step toward establishing a healing lifestyle is practicing the art of observing yourself. Observation keeps us present and allows us to understand what's going on in our own nervous system at any point in time. Bear in mind that observation does not include the intent of solving a problem now. We observe to begin to recognize what we are actually experiencing here and now. We observe to keep ourselves away from the crutch of distraction. We observe to begin the process of connecting. Observing is the first step toward being present in our lives.

As we observe, we begin to build a relationship with ourselves. Think about how you connect with other people: you watch their actions and reactions, and engage based on those observations, right? We need to practice doing this same thing with ourselves and, in doing so, utilize the same balance of compassion and analysis we focus on others. We tend to think of intimacy as a quality we share in relationship with other people, but it's also important to build an intimate relationship with ourselves, and we do this by paying attention to ourselves, just as we do with others. For people who have been traumatized, though, this can be scary. If we are present with ourselves, we might also have to be present with pain.

If you are struggling to observe yourself, begin to practice by observing your environment. For many people, this is a less threatening way to come into the present moment. Use your senses to notice what's around you, to fully be there. And then, as you grow more accustomed to that, start to shift your focus to notice how the environment impacts you. Do the sounds you hear soothe you or make you jumpy? Are the smells triggering or relaxing?

Here's what I love about observation: it is available to us at any time. Sometimes, though, we ignore it by skipping over observation in favor of focusing on either problems or solutions. If something is uncomfortable, there has to be a problem, and that means we need a solution. What about, instead, just sitting with that sensation? Noticing it. Getting curious about what you are feeling in that moment.

Without exception, every single person who comes to me for therapy has experienced some sort of breach in their attachment with themselves. This happens for a multitude of different reasons, some of which my patients will never consciously understand because breaches in attachment can occur during the preverbal years, including in utero or during birth. While this is not always the case, it is certainly not uncommon. Figuring out how to create this relationship with self is essential. It's ultimately the only way to find a sense of safety and autonomy. And it all starts with incorporating the power of observation in our own lives and toward our own selves on a regular, day-to-day basis.

As you begin to build the practice of observing yourself, it will become easier and easier to discern what is and isn't right to you. In fact, over time, the process will become so habitual that you won't even notice it's happening. You will become attuned with yourself, what you feel, and what you need. Once you have a greater sense of yourself, you can begin connecting to what makes you feel comfortable and uncomfortable, and cultivate a life that feels safer and much more meaningful.

### EXPERIENCE EMBODIMENT

As you become more aware of and present in your own experience, you will begin to drop deeper into your body. While we all have a body, a shocking number of us don't actually live in it. Without truly taking part in the physical experience of being a human being, we miss out on so much. We miss out on cues. We miss out on knowing what we need in order to feel safe. We miss out on vitality, joy, and the ability to live life in a more expansive and connected way.

Begin by finding safe ways of moving or feeling your body. You can think of these as entry points into your physical experience. Maybe it feels good to dance or go for a brisk walk. If you are over mobilized, see if you can slow yourself down and learn how to feel your body in a more relaxed state. Perhaps it feels good to relax in a restorative yoga pose, such as child's pose. Wherever that safe place of movement is for you, go there. And while you are feeling safe, begin to notice what's happening in your body.

Experiencing your body in these safe movements will help build resilience and a sense of tolerance so that you can also remain aware in your body during those moments when you feel unsafe or when old trauma is triggered. The way through the lingering echoes of trauma that ring throughout your nervous system is gaining a sense of mastery over those feelings in your body that you are avoiding or feeling too intensely. Trauma makes us feel threatened and, of course, we all want to avoid threats. But lingering trauma is no more than an outdated feeling that exists in our body. We move through and beyond it by allowing ourselves to experience it. By doing this, we learn that we can survive; that the sense of threat is not real. It's simply outdated information that continues to live within us.

## INCORPORATE LITTLE EXPERIMENTS

While observation and embodiment are essential elements of establishing a healing lifestyle, creating this lifestyle is also largely an exercise in choosing your own adventure. Again, no one is more of an expert on you than you are.

To do this, ingest the information that you are learning about yourself as you observe and move through the world in a state of increased awareness and attention. Notice the reactions that cause you discomfort or make your life more difficult. Notice where you feel some expansion, even if these moments are far and few between. I promise they will become more frequent and available over time as you continue to exercise the muscles of your nervous system. Think back to the assessments in Chapter Five and what you might have learned about yourself through them. For example, if you know that you tend to rely on rigid behaviors, invite yourself to do little experiments that slowly move you away from that state. One day that might include not making your bed; another day might involve going about your daily routine in a different order than usual. These little things are titrating you. If you go through life with a sense of rigidity in order to maintain a sense of control and keep things together, these tiny, low-stakes exercises might help you realize that everything doesn't fall apart if you let go a little. And, in fact, you might even realize that you feel a bit more relaxed when you allow yourself to loosen up a little.

To identify these inroads to healing in your own life, notice those places where it feels like you can create a little bit more fluidity or flexibility. Your ultimate goal is to create more freedom and space in your life, even if this happens by very small measures. And, in fact, it *should* happen in small measures, because those are more likely to be tolerable and, thus, sustainable.

## CREATE A SAFE SPACE

When we have a space of our own that feels safe, things shift. We feel more productive and empowered. Creating a safe space can also provide a sense of accomplishment because it is a personal expression of who you are and what you need to thrive.

While your home should be a safe space, you can also create a portable sensory toolkit that allows you to orient and feel safe (for more on this, refer back to Chapter 6). You can establish a sense of safety wherever you are. Perhaps you carry a tactile item with you that helps to soothe your anxiety simply by holding it. Maybe your safety comes from an intangible practice you can take anywhere with you, such as breath work. You might listen to music or have something visual to help you drop into a pleasant image. It could be that cooking is a safe space for you. If so, you can use this as a means of easing into greater social engagement by putting yourselves in situations where you can occupy yourself with cooking while interacting.

The options are endless, but the important thing is that you know what these safety tools are *before* you need them. Get curious and experiment with your senses. I have seen this cumulatively amount to huge shifts and transformations in my clients, because it allows them to engage and build resiliency in situations that might have previously been intolerable.

## HEALTHY SOCIAL ENGAGEMENT

A healing lifestyle begins with ourselves but, of course, vibrant and joyful life also requires social engagement. As you begin to feel safer within and more attached to yourself, you will find that you naturally begin to create healthier, more stable-feeling connections and attachments to others. As your nervous system starts to heal through observation, embodiment, and moving away from programmed behaviors, you see not only yourself but also the world around you more accurately. This means that you can more properly gauge which people and relationships are healthy for you and which are not.

Often, people who have experienced trauma fall into one of two extremes: patterns of isolation or over-attaching to others. These patterns can be difficult to break. And this is why it is important to begin with small measures. I'm not suggesting that you go out to a party or networking event and collect phone numbers or begin to detach from people you feel very connected to. Instead, notice the desire to isolate or over-attach when it arises, and see what it feels like to approach each situation differently. Perhaps you choose to go out for a walk and notice the people around you instead of isolating or heading straight for your go-to person. Then, after practicing this for a little while, you might begin to engage with others a bit more by making eye contact, then smiling, then saying hello. Again, we are looking for small steps we can incorporate to build over time to a healthier way of living.

## BEWARE OF IMPULSES

As you are working toward creating a healing lifestyle, pay attention to impulses. Impulses tend to arise because we don't want to be in a state of discomfort and our impulsive desires or behaviors offer us a way out. An impulsive desire such as "I need ice cream *now*" is often just the reaction to "I can't tolerate the way I feel in my body."

The next time you notice that you are feeling a strong impulse, practice stopping for a moment and recognizing what discomfort you are trying to avoid. Then ask yourself if instead of following that impulse you can instead lean into the discomfort, even for a short amount of time.

Maybe you can wait another ten minutes before going for that ice cream. Or maybe, in a different circumstance, rather than fleeing a party immediately, you can recognize that you feel uncomfortable and ask yourself to stay for another two minutes despite that.

Impulsiveness is avoidance. By nature, impulses feel urgent, but the second you call out that false sense of security for what it is, you can begin to practice new behaviors. You can think of impulses as little windows presenting themselves to you so that you can keep cracking them open a little bit wider, opening up more and more room for healing to stream into your life.

## ONLY YOU HAVE THE ANSWERS

The more we can observe ourselves, the more we provide ourselves with the space and opportunity to move through experiences in a new way. The more we can be aware of the ways in which there is room to live a healthier, more fulfilling, and more free life.

In so many other areas of life today, we're told that the cultivating healthier behavior involves *more* of something: exercise more, focus more, eat more of the right things. As you feel into your own experience, you may find that, for you, a healthier life does include more of something. However, for a lot of us, it requires less of something. And, in some cases, it even involves nothing of something. For example, if you are a person who tends to run on overdrive, the healthiest thing you can incorporate into your life is, well, more of nothing.

But, again, no one knows what you need precisely except for you. Your therapist doesn't know, and I don't know. It is your own observance of yourself and the ability to allow yourself to feel what you are feeling that will ultimately lead you down a healing path. This is a practice we can all cultivate on a day by day, moment by moment basis.

# CONCLUSION

While it is important that each of us has the opportunity for our story to be heard, there is a balance. Repeating the same story over and over and over again will not ultimately result in healing; in fact, it can often result in re-traumatization. Not to mention the fact that our stories ultimately only tell us so much.

We fall into this pattern of getting stuck in the story, first of all, because that's what traditional therapy tells us to do. And, second of all, because we're trying to take control of our story by telling it. However, true healing and autonomy come from developing a new relationship with our past. What did we learn from the story? What good things came from it? How did it make us stronger? While the facts are the facts, it is how we integrate and renegotiate with the past that helps us move forward.

When we approach healing from a body-based per-spective, we are given the opportunity to release our story—which, for so many of us, becomes a part of our identity—and the ongoing hold it has on our nervous system. We have a new ability to write our next chapter.

I hope that you will take this book as an invitation to begin experiencing your own body. What is it telling you? Where are you holding on to trauma? How is that trauma impacting your daily life? And how might you be able to let it go by allowing yourself to feel it and, from there, build a new sense of safety? This is what healing looks like.

This process inherently involves our body because it is intricately connected with our mind. As human beings, we are holistic creatures, and we are never going to heal by working exclusively from the neck up. Remember, your nervous system does not function through thoughts; it functions through feelings. So many of us are not able to feel these feelings because we have, at one point or another, given up our relationship with ourselves. At some point in time, detachment felt like the safest option. It was a way of escaping emotional discomfort.

To resolve this and reattach and rebuild that relationship for our healing, we have to find a way to become more comfortable with the discomfort. Over time as we begin to heal, that discomfort will melt away—but not until we allow ourselves to check back in our body and experience it. This is not a cognitive process; it's a physical one.

As we heal through physical presence, our relationship with ourselves becomes stronger and safer. Once we reach this point, we can trust ourselves to engage in relationships with others without compromising ourselves in the process. This new attunement with our body ensures that our newly calibrated nervous system simply won't allow for that to happen. If a warning shot is fired off, we will notice it through our presence and react accordingly.

This opens us up to experience the world through an entirely new perspective. We get to exercise our autonomy in an entirely new way and this, in turn, leads to a sense of empowerment and resilience. It is for this reason that healing allows us such a greater capacity to thrive and experience joy in our lives. We can live more spontaneously, with more ease and fluidity. We can allow life to unfold and reveal itself, confident that we are capable and strong enough to handle whatever comes our way.

Perhaps everything in this book doesn't resonate with you, and that's okay. I would invite you to simply get curious about those elements that do. Curiosity leads us to a more playful place and that, in and of itself, is healing. It's where we can discover new ways of being.

# REFERENCES

Amali, S., Chowdhury, S., & Pychyl, T. (2017). The Relation between
Affect Intensity and Procrastination. *Psicologia Di Comunita'*,
*1*(1), 11–23.

Armstrong, J. G., Putnam, F. W., Carlson, E. B., Libero, D. Z., &
Smith, S. R. (1997). Development and Validation of a Measure
of Adolescent Dissociation: The Adolescent Dissociative
Experiences Scale. *The Journal of Nervous and Mental Disease*,
*185*(8), 491.

Aron, E. N., & Aron, A. (1997). Sensory-processing sensitivity
and its relation to introversion and emotionality. *Journal of
Personality and Social Psychology*, *73*(2), 345–368.

Ayres, A. J., & Robbins, J. (2005). *Sensory Integration and the Child:
Understanding Hidden Sensory Challenges*. Los Angeles, CA:
Western Psychological Services.

Baldwin, D. (2013). Primitive mechanisms of trauma response:
An evolutionary perspective on trauma-related disorders.
*Neuroscience and Biobehavioral Reviews*, *37*, 1549–1566.

Baranek, G. T., David, F. J., Poe, M. D., Stone, W. L., & Watson, L. R. (2006). Sensory Experiences Questionnaire: Discriminating sensory features in young children with autism, developmental delays, and typical development: SEQ. *Journal of Child Psychology and Psychiatry*, 47(6), 591-601.

Beauchaine, T. (2001). Vagal tone, development, and Gray's motivational theory: Toward an integrated model of autonomic nervous system functioning in psychopathology. *Development and Psychopathology*, 13(2), 183-214.

Beauchaine, T. P., Gatzke-Kopp, L., & Mead, H. K. (2007). Polyvagal Theory and developmental psychopathology: Emotion dysregulation and conduct problems from preschool to adolescence. *Biological Psychology*, 74(2), 174-184.

Becker, W. J., & Cropanzano, R. (2010). Organizational neuroscience: The promise and prospects of an emerging discipline—Becker—2010—Journal of Organizational Behavior—Wiley Online Library. *Journal of Organizational Behavior*, 31, 1055-1059.

Becker, W. J., & Cropanzano, R. (2010). Organizational neuroscience: The promise and prospects of an emerging discipline. *Journal of Organizational Behavior*, 31, 1055-1059.

Ben-Avi, N., Almagor, M., & Engel-Yeger, B. (2012). Sensory Processing Difficulties and Interpersonal Relationships in Adults: An Exploratory Study. *Psychology*, 3(1), 70-77.

Blaustein, M., Cook, A., Cloitre, M., DeRosa, R., Ford, J., Henderson, M., ... van der Kolk, B. (2003). *Complex Trauma in Children and Adolescents* [White Paper]. Retrieved May 15, 2019, from National Child Traumatic Stress Network: https://www. nctsn.org/sites/default/files/resources/complex_trauma_in_ children_and_adolescents.pdf

Bracha, H. S. (2004). Freeze, Flight, Fight, Fright, Faint: Adaptationist Perspectives on the Acute Stress Response Spectrum. *CNS Spectrums*, 9(9), 679-685.

Briere, J. N., & Runtz, M. G. (1989). The Trauma Symptom Checklist (TSC-33): Early data on a new scale. *Journal of Interpersonal Violence, 4*, 151–163.

Brown, C., Tollefson, N., Dunn, W., Cromwell, R., & Filion, D. (2001). The Adult Sensory Profile: Measuring Patterns of Sensory Processing. *The American Journal of Occupational Therapy, 55*, 75–82.

Ceunen, E., Vlaeyen, J., & Van Diest, I. (2016). On the Origin of Interoception. *Frontiers in Psychology, 7*, 1–17.

Clancy, K., Ding, M., Bernat, E., Schmidt, N. B., & Li, W. (2017). Restless 'rest': Intrinsic sensory hyperactivity and disinhibition in post-traumatic stress disorder. *Brain, 140*(7), 2041–2050.

Corrigan, F., Fisher, J., & Nutt, D. (2011). Autonomic dysregulation and the Window of Tolerance model of the effects of complex emotional trauma. *Journal of Psychopharmacology, 25*(1), 17–25.

Craig, A. D. (2003). Interoception: The sense of the physiological condition of the body. *Current Opinion in Neurobiology, 13*(4), 500–505.

Common Reactions After Trauma. (2018). National Center for PTSD, U.S. Department of Veteran's Affairs. Retrieved from https://www.ptsd.va.gov/understand/isitptsd/common_reactions.asp

Corr, P. J., & Cooper, A. J. (2016). The Reinforcement Sensitivity Theory of Personality Questionnaire (RST-PQ): Development and validation. *Psychological Assessment, 28*(11), 1427–1440.

Damasio, A. (2003). Feelings of Emotion and the Self. *Annals of the New York Academy of Sciences, 1001*, 253–261.

Dunn, W. (2007). Supporting Children to Participate Successfully in Everyday Life by Using Sensory Processing Knowledge. *Infants & Young Children, 20*(2), 84.

Eckert, M., Ebert, D., Lehr, D., Sieland, B., & Berking, M. (2016). Overcome procrastination: Enhancing emotion regulation skills reduce procrastination—ScienceDirect. *Learning and Individual Differences, 52*, 10-18.

Engel-Yeger, B., Palgy-Levin, D., & Lev-Wiesel, R. (2013). The Sensory Profile of People with Post-Traumatic Stress Symptoms. *Occupational Therapy in Mental Health, 29*(3), 266-278.

Foa, E., Ehlers, A., Clark, D. M., Tomlin, D. F., & Orsillo, S. M. (1999). The Posttraumatic Cognitions Inventory (PTCI): Development and Validation. *Psychological Assessment, 11*(3), 303-314.

Glick, D. A., Millstein, D. J., & Orsillo, S. M. (2014). A preliminary investigation of the role of psychological inflexibility in academic procrastination—ScienceDirect. *Journal of Contextual Behavioral Science, 3*(2), 81-88.

Gottlieb, G., Wahlsten, D., & Lickliter, R. (2006). The Significance of Biology for Human Development: A Developmental Psychobiological Systems View. In R. M. Lerner (Ed.), *Handbook of Child Psychology, Volume 1: Theoretical Models of Human Development* (6th ed., pp. 210-257). Hoboken, NJ: John Wiley & Sons, Inc.

Gratz, K. L., & Roemer, L. (2004). Multidimensional Assessment of Emotion Regulation and Dysregulation: Development, Factor Structure, and Initial Validation of the Difficulties in Emotion Regulation Scale. *Journal of Psychopathology and Behavioral Assessment, 26*(1), 41-54.

Hammad, M. A., Barsky, A. J., & Regestein, Q. R. (2001). Correlation Between Somatic Sensation Inventory Scores and Hyperarousal Scale Scores. *Psychosomatics, 42*(1), 29-34.

Harshaw, C. (2015). Interoceptive Dysfunction: Toward An Integrated Framework for Understanding Somatic and Affective Disturbance in Depression. *Psychological Bulletin, 141*(2), 311-363.

Hebert, K. R. (2016). The association between sensory processing styles and mindfulness. *British Journal of Occupational Therapy*, *79*(9), 557–564.

Helping Patients Cope With A Traumatic Event. (n.d.) Centers for Disease Control. Retrieved from https://www.cdc.gov/masstrauma/factsheets/professionals/coping_professional.pdf

Jackson, C. J. (2009). Jackson-5 scales of revised Reinforcement Sensitivity Theory (r-RST) and their application to dysfunctional real world outcomes. *Journal of Research in Personality*, *43*(4), 556–569.

James, K., Miller, L. J., Schaaf, R., Nielsen, D. M., & Schoen, S. A. (2011). Phenotypes within sensory modulation dysfunction. *Comprehensive Psychiatry*, *52*(6), 715–724.

Jerome, E. M., & Liss, M. (2005). Relationships between sensory processing style, adult attachment, and coping. *Personality and Individual Differences*, *38*(6), 1341–1352.

Kinnealey, M., Koenig, K. P., & Smith, S. (2011). Relationships Between Sensory Modulation and Social Supports and Health-Related Quality of Life. *American Journal of Occupational Therapy*, *65*(3), 320–327.

Kozlowska, K., Walker, P., McLean, L., & Carrive, P. (2015). Fear and the Defense Cascade: Clinical Implications and Management. *Harvard Review of Psychiatry*, *23*(4), 263–287.

Leith, K. P., & Baumeister, R. (1996). Why do bad moods increase self-defeating behavior? Emotion, risk tasking, and self-regulation. *Journal of Personality and Social Psychology*, *71*(6), 1250–1267.

Levine, P. (2010). *In an Unspoken Voice: How the Body Releases Trauma and Restores Goodness*. Berkeley, CA: North Atlantic Books.

Lickliter, R. (2011). The Integrated Development of Sensory Organization. *Clinics in Perinatology, 38*(4), 591–603.

Ma-Kellams, C. (2014). Cross-cultural differences in somatic awareness and interoceptive accuracy: A review of the literature and directions for future research. *Frontiers in Psychology, 5*, 1–9.

Mehling, W. (2016). Differentiating attention styles and regulatory aspects of self-reported interoceptive sensibility. *Philosophical Transactions of the Royal Society B: Biological Sciences, 371*, 1–11.

Mehling, W. E., Acree, M., Stewart, A., Silas, J., & Jones, A. (2018). The Multidimensional Assessment of Interoceptive Awareness, Version 2 (MAIA-2). *PLOS ONE, 13*(12), e0208034.

Morris, L., & Mansell, W. (2018). A systematic review of the relationship between rigidity/flexibility and transdiagnostic cognitive and behavioral processes that maintain psychopathology. *Journal of Experimental Psychopathology, July–September*, 1–40.

Nock, M. K., Wedig, M. M., Holmberg, E. B., & Hooley, J. M. (2008). The Emotion Reactivity Scale: Development, Evaluation, and Relation to Self-Injurious Thoughts and Behaviors. *Behavior Therapy, 39*(2), 107–116.

Rosenberg, S. (2017). *Accessing the healing power of the vagus nerve: Self-help exercises for anxiety, depression, trauma, and autism.* Berkeley, CA: North Atlantic Books.

Ogden, P., Minton, K., & Pain, C. (2006). *Trauma and the body: A sensorimotor approach to psychotherapy.* New York: W.W. Norton.

Payne, P., Levine, P. A., & Crane-Godreau, M. A. (2015). Somatic experiencing: Using interoception and proprioception as core elements of trauma therapy. *Frontiers in Psychology, 6*, 1–18.

Porges, S. W. (2011). *The polyvagal theory: Neurophysiological foundations of emotions, attachment, communication, and self-regulation.* New York: W.W. Norton.

Rash, J., & Aguirre-Camacho, A. (2012). Attention-deficit hyperactivity disorder and cardiac vagal control: A systematic review. *ADHD Attention Deficit and Hyperactivity Disorders, 4*(4), 167–177.

Roelofs, K. (2017). Freeze for action: Neurobiological mechanisms in animal and human freezing. *Philosophical Transactions of the Royal Society B: Biological Sciences, 372,* 1–10.

Rose, S. (2014). The key to keeping your balance is knowing when you've lost it. *British Journal of Psychotherapy Integration, 11*(1), 29–41.

Rose, S. A., Sheffield, D., & Harling, M. (2018). The Integration of the Workable Range Model into a Mindfulness-Based Stress Reduction Course: A Practice-Based Case Study. *Mindfulness, 9*(2), 430–440.

Scaer, R. C. (2001). The Neurophysiology of Dissociation and Chronic Disease. *Applied Psychophysiology and Biofeedback, 26*(1), 73–91.

Schauer, M., & Elbert, T. (2010). Dissociation Following Traumatic Stress: Etiology and Treatment. *Zeitschrift Für Psychologie / Journal of Psychology, 218*(2), 109–127.

Siegel, D. J. (2010). *Mindsight: The new science of personal transformation.* New York: Bantam Books.

Sirois, F., & Giguère, B. (2018). Giving in when feeling less good: Procrastination, action control, and social temptations. *British Journal of Social Psychology, 57*(2), 404–427.

Smederevac, S., Mitrović, D., Čolović, P., & Nikolašević, Ž. (2014). Validation of the Measure of Revised Reinforcement Sensitivity Theory Constructs. *Journal of Individual Differences, 35*(1), 12–21.

Substance Abuse and Mental Health Services Administration. (2014). *Trauma-Informed Care in Behavioral Health Services. Treatment Improvement Protocol (TIP) Series 57.* HHS Publication No. (SMA) 13-4801. Rockville, MD: Substance Abuse and Mental Health Services Administration. Retrieved from https://www.integration.samhsa.gov/clinical-practice/SAMSA_TIP_Trauma.pdf

Steel, P. (2007). The nature of procrastination: A meta-analytic and theoretical review of quintessential self-regulatory failure. *Psychological Bulletin, 133*(1), 65–94.

Stupiggia, M. (2012). From Hopeless Solitude to the Sense of Being-With: Functions and Dysfunctions of Mirror Neurons in Post Traumatic Syndromes. *International Body Psychotherapy Journal, 11*(1), 25–40.

Tavassoli, T., Miller, L. J., Schoen, S. A., Nielsen, D. M., & Baron-Cohen, S. (2014). Sensory over-responsivity in adults with autism spectrum conditions. *Autism, 18*(4), 428–432.

Tomchek, S. D., & Dunn, W. (2007). Sensory Processing in Children With and Without Autism: A Comparative Study Using the Short Sensory Profile. *American Journal of Occupational Therapy, 61,* 190–200.

Van der Kolk, B. A. (2014). *The body keeps the score: Brain, mind, and body in the healing of trauma.* New York: Viking.

Volchan, E., Rocha-Rego, V., Bastos, A. F., Oliveira, J. M., Franklin, C., Gleiser, S., ... Figueira, I. (2017). Immobility reactions under threat: A contribution to human defensive cascade and PTSD. *Neuroscience & Biobehavioral Reviews, 76,* 29–38.

Zelen, S. L., & Levitt, E. E. (1954). Notes on the Wesley Rigidity Scale: The development of a short form. *The Journal of Abnormal and Social Psychology, 49*(3), 472–473.

# ACKNOWLEDGMENTS

I want to thank my best friend Tami and my family, especially my brother David and sister in law, Anna, for holding a safe space for me through the toughest time of my life. I would and could not have made it this far without all of your love and support.

Thank you to Sarah Melancon for all of your hard work, dedication, and expertise in the research and creation of the assessment scales included in these pages. Sarah, this book could not have happened without your contribution.

Additionally, I want to thank Claire Winters and Nikki Van Noy for the amazing collaboration in making this book happen.

# ABOUT THE AUTHOR

ILENE SMITH is a Certified Professional Coach (CPC) through the GROW Training Institute, Inc. and holds a Master's degree in both Mental Health Counseling and Exercise Physiology. She is also a Somatic Experiencing Practitioner (SEP) and completed a three-year training with the Somatic Experiencing Institute founded by trauma therapy pioneer Peter Levine.

Ilene's work is rooted in the principles of Somatic Experiencing (SE), attachment theory, and bodynamics. Her training in trauma healing provides the foundation to help clients resolve trauma symptoms and relieve chronic stress and pain in the body. Integrating several modalities into her practice, including talking, touch work, and movement, Ilene is able to support the body tissue memory and nervous system to create synergy between body and mind. Her work supports clients in developing a deeper and safer relationship within and ultimately greater capacity for resilience and joy. Clients move from a state of rigidity to a life of fluidity, ease, and vitality. Through her extensive studies in physiology and nervous system regulation, Ilene has developed techniques and methods to safely bring clients from trauma states back into a new and empowered body. The result of this process is freedom and expansion, which allows clients to experience autonomy and self-respect.

Learn more at ilenesmith.com.

Made in the USA
Coppell, TX
08 May 2023

16585718R00152